INSIGHT POCKET GUIDES

GRAN Canaria

Inselführer Gran Canaria

KW-050-706

APA PUBLICATIONS

Part of the Langenscheidt Publishing Group

L

The Canary Islands

120 km / 75 miles

Atlantic Ocean

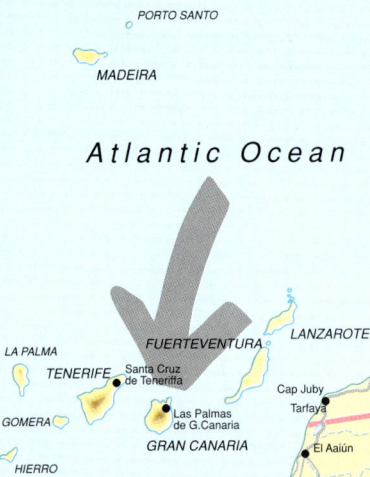

Pontevedra
Ponferrada
Valladolid
Zamora
Porto
Duero
Salamanca
Vila Nova de Gaia
Avila
Covilhã
Talavera de la Reina
Punta Monego
Emb. de Alcántara
S P A I N
Coimbra
Cáceres
Punta Carvoeiro
Mérida
Don Benito
P O R T U G A L
Lisboa
Badajoz
Almada
Córdoba
Alcácer do Sul
Punta Espichel
Galaroza
Punta de Sines
Beja
Sevilla
Odemira
ALGARVE
Huelva
Jerez de la Frontera
Ajamonte
Punta de São Vicente
Faro
Sagres
GULF OF CÁDIZ
Cádiz
Gibraltar
Strait of Gibraltar
Tanger
Tétouar
Larache
Kenitra
Fès
Salé
Rabat
Meknès
Casablanca
Dar- el- Beida
Quedzem
El- Jadida (Mazagan)
Settat
Benimellal
Safi
M O R O C C O
Essaouira
Marrakesh
Jebel Toubkal 4165
Zagora
Taroudant
Agadir
A T L A S
Bouizakarn
PORTO SANTO
MADEIRA
Atlantic Ocean
Cap Dráa
LANZAROTE
Tantan
A L G E R I A
LA PALMA
FUERTEVENTURA
Cap Juby
Tindouf
TENERIFE
Santa Cruz de Teneriffa
Tarfaya
Las Palmas de G.Canaria
GOMERA
GRAN CANARIA
El Aiún
W E S T E R N
S A H A R A
HIERRO
M A U R I T A N I A

Welcome!

Known by the ancient Greeks as the 'makaron nesoi' (Fortunate Islands) and by the Romans as the Land of Eternal Spring, the Canary Islands have always seemed to exist more in myth than in reality. Though Spanish, they lie 100km (62 miles) adrift from the coast of Africa, some 1,000km (620 miles) from Spain. The most diverse of the islands is Gran Canaria, the subject of this guide. While people bask in the sun at Playa del Inglés, its most popular resort, snow can cap the peaks at Tejeda, 40km (25 miles) inland.

In these pages, Insight's correspondent on Gran Canaria, Margaret Hart, has devised a series of itineraries linking the island's highlights: the first seven are devoted to Las Palmas and the north and the remaining four concentrate on the attractions of the south, taking the resort of Playa del Inglés as a base. Supporting the itineraries are sections on history and culture, shopping, eating out and nightlife, as well as a calendar of special events and a practical information section providing vital tips.

Margaret Hart has lived in Gran Canaria for around 15 years, earning her living as an interpreter and lecturer in tourism. In this guide her aim is to reveal the less publicised attractions of Gran Canaria, which even committed sunseekers come to admire most – if only they are introduced. She hopes to prise visitors off the island's sand and send them in search of its soul. That said, she has not neglected the justly famous beaches, which have been child-tested by her own two girls.

C O N T E N T S

Pages 2/3:
Puerto de las
Nieves

The South

The remaining itineraries in the guide are devoted to the south of Gran Canaria, where most of the main beach resorts are found. They use Playa del Inglés/Maspalomas as a base.

Pages 8/9: camel safari in the south

HISTORY & CULTURE

It is always difficult to separate the myth from the reality in the history and culture of the Canary Islands. Nobody is really clear what the Canary Islands were like before the 14th century, when the Spanish invaders finally put them on the geographical map and wiped the original Guanche culture off the face of the earth. If legend is anything to go by, Gran Canaria and its sister islands appear to have been a kind of pastoral Arcadia. Both the Greeks and Romans wrote about them in glowing terms, calling them the Hesperides, the Gardens of the Gods and Land of Eternal Spring and thereby, somewhat unwittingly, setting them firmly on their way to becoming the great tourist attractions they are today.

Nor are the geological origins of the islands free from mythical interpretations. For many, the islands represent the remains of the sunken continent of Atlantis. A slightly more scientific hypothesis maintains that they are parts of Africa which broke away and drifted

Myths – such as the tree which showered water – make up Canarian history

like ice floes in the shifting and sliding of the continents. The most extravagant of the hypotheses goes so far as to claim that the islands are the summits of a mountain chain which is still nosing its way upwards out of the Atlantic Ocean. What is known for certain is that they are volcanic islands, some of which are over 10 million years old.

Origins

The name 'Canary Islands' calls to mind the yellow song birds we like to keep in cages – but don't expect to find canaries fluttering around here. There are all sorts of theories on the origin of the name of the islands, but song birds don't feature in any of them.

The most commonly held theory is recorded by Pliny in his account of an exploratory expedition sent by King Juba II of Mauretania to the island of Gran Canaria. The expedition returned to Mauretania with two large dogs, the *canes* of Canaria. That the locals share this theory is apparent in their coat-of-arms, emblazoned with two dogs, and the bronze sculptures of dogs that grace the Plaza de Santa Ana in Las Palmas (*see Itinerary 1, page 23*).

Dogs gave the islands their name

However, there are no such doubts as to the origins of the 'Gran' in Gran Canaria. The heroic and stubborn defence of the island led the Spanish invaders to christen it 'Great'. For a long time, the Spaniards struggled to conquer the island, their difficulty largely due to the 14 local chieftains, the *guanartemes*, who rallied together together to stave off the enemy attacks. On the other Canary Islands the leaders were divided among themselves, making the Spaniards' job much easier. Again, if legend is to be believed, the unity encountered on Gran Canaria was the work of Princess Andamana of Gáldar, a woman of potent charm who seduced all 14 chieftains, thereby giving them something in common to fight for, and then married her blood brother to avoid causing rifts between her former suitors. On the other islands, in contrast, the women tended to fall prey to the Spaniards' charms and helped them in their conquest – particularly on El Hierro, the smallest of the Canary Islands.

Gran Canaria also fares favourably in etymological comparisons with the other islands, especially with Tenerife, which was originally known as Hell, possibly because Teide, the island's highest mountain, was then an active volcano.

11

Death of a Culture

Faced with the inevitability of defeat by the Spanish, the *guanartemes* on Gran Canaria decided to end it all rather than live in slavery. Their method of death was as drastic as it was spectacular: they threw themselves off the highest rockfaces of the island. Those who survived the invasion quickly adapted to their new circumstances. The Guanches were, after all, a peace-loving, law-abiding race of cave-dwellers who divided their time between their communal fields and their herds of goats. Their two games of skill were not at all warlike in nature – the *juego del garrote* (two opponents armed with shepherds' crooks) and the *lucha canaria* (a kind of wrestling match) were only played to pass the time when they were not singing or dancing.

Their God was *Alcorán*, the God of the Sky, and their religion was based on fertility rites and rainmaking ceremonies. The two sacred mountains of Humiaga (now Cuatro Puertas: see *Itineraries*) and Tirma were used as *harimaguadas*, sanctuaries for the virgin daughters of their nobility. Before being married off, these girls were taken to special grain stores, such as the Cenobio de Valerón, to be fattened for the event. These young women were highly important in the Guanche culture since it was through them that the race was perpetuated. According to legend, in Gomera and Gran Canaria it was customary for a man to 'gift' his wife to a visiting guest in order to introduce new blood into the family.

The Spanish invaders described the Guanche men as exceedingly tall and the women as incredibly beautiful. Though it should be remembered that the average Spaniard of the time was no giant and that the soldiers had been a long time at sea without clapping eyes on a woman, the evidence does actually indicate that the Spaniards might have been right: mummies on display in the Museo Canario in Las Palmas are around 1.84m (6ft) tall, certainly way above the average of the time.

The process of mummification was elaborate. It involved disembowelling the corpse, bathing it in shallow salt water (the Guanches apparently did not swim), then leaving it to dry, after which the body was wrapped in goatskins and buried in

A Guanche mummy

one of a number of ways, depending upon social rank. The sap of the *drago*, the dragon tree indigenous to the islands, seems to have played an essential part in this ritual. Called 'dragon's blood' on account of its reddish colour, the sap was held to possess miraculous healing properties – which is probably just as well since the Guanches' other important form of medical treatment was *trepanación* – a hole in the head.

Roots and Politics

To all intents and purposes, the culture of the Guanches disappeared after the Conquest and the subsequent incorporation of the island into the Spanish kingdom of the Catholic Monarchs, Ferdinand

The Spaniards brought Christianity

and Isabella, in 1478. Unfortunately there were no written records of the original language, which is thought to have been of Berber (African) origin. Canary Spanish is very different from mainland Spanish but this is only to be expected of islands which are nearer Africa than Spain and have received influxes of people from all parts of the world. Moreover many Canarios who migrated to various parts of Latin America, above all Venezuela and Cuba, later returned to their beloved islands with new words and phrases. Words such as *naife* (knife) or *guagua* (bus) only exist here, so even mainland Spaniards sometimes have trouble understanding the islanders.

Short-lived attempts have been made to dig out cultural roots and restore the lost Guanche identity, mainly by artists and intellectuals. The most important work has been done by the Millares family, above all the painter Manolo Millares. Other influential figures include the sculptor Martin Chirino, who has incorporated the symbols of the *pintaderas* (the wooden or terracotta seals of the Guanches) into his work; Tony Gallardo, who works mainly with volcanic rock; the Padorno brothers; and the outspoken lady artist, Lola Massien.

Political movements of a nationalistic nature have only recently become popular on the island. Up until the beginning of the 1990s, the people of Gran Canaria, in particular, had tended to be middle-of-the-road in their politics. Indeed, the only seat won by the Central Democratic Pary in the whole of Spain in elections in 1990 was in Gran Canaria. In the early 1970s there was a spate of bomb

Typical dress in the 1830s

scares mainly stage-managed by the lawyer Antonio Cubillo and his radically nationalistic political party, MPAIAC. Exiled at the time in Algeria, Cubillo used to broadcast political propaganda over the radio and became an almost mythical figure. But democracy has changed all that and Cubillo is now considered an anecdotal and picturesque figure from the past.

However, the traditional rivalry between the two major islands of Gran Canaria and Tenerife, the latter presently ruled by a virulently insular party, has led to greater interest in local parties, although Gran Canaria always opts for the major national parties when it comes to the crunch.

A Bridge Between Continents

The Canary Islands have long been important as a strategic port of call. Columbus stopped off here at least once en route to America. The strong trading links which were established between the Canary Islands, Europe, America and Africa were to bring people of all nations to these shores. At the time when sugar cultivation was booming in the south of the island (at Agüimes and Ingenio, for example) slaves were brought here, mainly by the Portuguese, from Africa. Thus, in Gran Canaria, there are two distinctly different strains of people: the tall, slender fair-skinned Canary islanders (the original Guanches were said to be redheads) and the swarthy, dark-skinned wiry-haired mainlanders. Although the ancient custom of gifting the wife no longer exists, the introduction of 'new blood' by people from all parts of the world is apparent – above all on islands such as Fuerteventura where blonde-haired locals were non-existent before tourism.

Columbus is remembered here

Hotel patio from the early days of tourism

The first and most important settlers were the British who originally came for reasons of health. One of the first tourist guides was Samler Brown's *Madeira, Canary Islands and Azores: A Practical and Complete Guide for the use of Tourists and Invalids* published in 1898. The British are held in great esteem by the Gran Canarians because their presence on the island has proved highly beneficial. For a long time Britain was the main foreign market for the principal exports from Gran Canaria, cochineal and wine. And when the other crops were blighted by plagues or foreign competition, the British introduced the cultivation of bananas and tomatoes.

Miller and Elder, whose warehouses still stand in the Parque Santa Catalina in Las Palmas, were largely responsible for opening up and developing the import-export trade which eventually prompted the Spanish government to nominate Las Palmas a Free Trade port. The water and electricity supplies were also set up by the British. Moreover, the second staple food of the Canary islanders (*gofio*, toasted cornflour, is the first) is the potato or *papa* which was grown from British seed – though an Englishman today would be hard-put to recognise the King Edward potato in the spud the Canaries call *papa kinewa*!

Cosmopolitan Community

Tourism, which represents a somewhat unbalanced 80 percent of the total income and employment of the island, has gradually brought people from all parts of the world to Gran Canaria – and a great many have stayed, attracted by the benign climate and, above all, the easy-going pace of life and the hospitality of the local community. There are Japanese, German, British and French schools on the island – and even a community of Korean nuns. Although the times

15

when the people of Gran Canaria left their front doors open at night and invited complete strangers to share their meals are things of the past, the most lasting impression that visitors take away is of the extraordinary hospitality of this island.

Nevertheless, as in the times of their forefathers, the people of Gran Canaria reveal a united front when faced with people who have come here merely to make a quick killing from the tourist business. Such people are given the derogatory title of *godos* (Goths) by the islanders and it is not unusual to see rubbish bins sprayed with the words *Godos aquí* ('deposit Goths here').

Gran Canarians view the gradual process of integration into the EU with mixed feelings: on the one hand, they are enthusiastic about belonging to the European Union – perhaps more so than mainland Spaniards – but on the other fear the economic consequences for the islands, which some predict the Community will ignore. In any event, as has been the case in the past, the islanders are likely to adapt cheerfully to the new set of circumstances and strive to maintain the quality of the peaceful life they have long defended. Gran Canaria has the added status of the archipelago's capital – Las Palmas de Gran Canaria – although the administration is shared with Santa Cruz in Tenerife.

Although the pace of life is easy-going and the temperature is a balmy 22°C (71°F) average all year round, inviting visitors to lie back and relax, this does not mean that Gran Canaria is not moving with the times. The major facelift undergone by Las Palmas de Gran Canaria in the mid-1990s, the plans afoot for development as an off-shore trading zone, and large-scale building projects such as the new auditorium and convention centres show that Gran Canaria is moving determinedly into the 21st century.

Tourism produces 80 percent of island income

Historical Highlights

BC The Greeks and the Romans mention the Canary Islands in their texts. They refer to them as the *makaron nesoi*, the Gardens of the Hesperides, the Land of Eternal Spring and the Fortunate Islands. At that time, the islands were also probably known to the Phoenicians.

1st century AD Pliny writes of the expedition sent to the islands by King Juba II of Mauretania. The expedition brings back two enormous dogs. No mention is made of the islands being inhabited although the natives, the Guanches, may have hidden in caves to avoid detection, as has been proved in the case of the island of Lanzarote.

1367 The Canaries appear on a map for the first time since they were charted by Ptolemy in the the 2nd century AD.

1475–83 The island is constantly under attack, first by the Portuguese and then by the Spaniards under different leaders but financed by the Catholic Monarchs, Ferdinand and Isabella.

The whole island of Gran Canaria submits to Pedro de Vera in 1483. This is largely due to the help of Tenesor Semidan, a *guanarteme* from the north who is captured, baptised a Christian under the name of Fernando Guanarteme and help to convince his fellow islanders to surrender. Many of the other *guanartemes*, the local chieftains, throw themselves off the clifftops rather than submit.

1478 The first city, the Real de Las Palmas, is founded on Gran Canaria by the Crown of Castile.

1492 Christopher Columbus stops off here on his first voyage to the New World. He repairs the rudder of *La Pinta* and the sail of *La Niña* (between the 25 August and the 1 September, according to the logbook). He returns to Las Palmas on his second and fourth voyages.

15th and 16th centuries The Portuguese set up sugar plantations and mills in the south. They bring slaves from Africa. Attacks from Sir Francis Drake and the Dutch under Van der Hoes are repelled.

1526 Royal Tribunal established in Gran Canaria for the settlement of local disputes.

18th and 19th centuries The main exports are wine and cochineal. The British set up a consulate on the islands from 1856 onwards. British settlers lay down the foundations of the import/export trade and play a large part in achieving water and electricity supplies. Coaling stations are set up in the harbour area to refuel transatlantic shipping.

1843 Benito Pérez Galdós, one of Spain's greatest novelists of all time, is born in Las Palmas de Gran Canaria.

1852 The islands are declared a Free Trade zone. The first tourists arrive on the islands.

1870s Gran Canaria still only has barely 10 miles of real road.

1927 The Canary Islands are divided into two provinces, East and West.

1936 Francisco Franco leaves Las Palmas for Spain and the Spanish Civil War begins.

1983 The Canary Islands are granted autonomous government but remain part of Spain.

1990 The island population reaches 600,000, with 355,000 living in the city of Las Palmas.

Gran Canaria

8 km / 5 miles

Atlantic Ocean

Punta de Gáldar

Punta de Guanarteme

Punta Sardina

Túmolo de la Guancha

PLAYA DE SARDINA

Ceno de Vale

Sardina del Norte

Gáldar

Cueva Pintada

Sta.Maria de Guia

San Isidor

Reptilandia

Punta de Cardonal

Cuevas de las Cruces

El Palm Vergarra

Agaete

Presa Bc. Hondo

Bascamao

Dedo de Diós

PLAYA SEGURA

Los Berrazales

Pinar de Tamabadar

1444

Punta de Góngora

El Risco

Mirador de Balcón

C.d.Tirma

Montaña Altavista

1376

Andén Verde

Mor

1

Puerto de la Aldea

Cruz de Teje

Punta de la Aldea

Presa del El Paralillo

Roque Bentaiga

Tejeda

Presa del Caidero de las Niñas

R N 1

San Nicolás de Tolentino

Los Molinos

El Toscon

Presa de Siberio

El Fraile

PLAYA DE GÜIGÜI

Inagua

1426

Cuevas de Pajonales

Cueva de las Niñas

Tasarte

El Descojonado

Las Casas de Veneguera

Presa de Soria

Embalse de Chira

PLAYA DE ASNO

Santa Brigida

Barranco de Tasarte

Pie de Cuesta

Punta Rabelago

Casas El Inglés

Barranco Veneguera

Mogán

La Playa de Veneguera

Tabaibales

La Playa de Mogán

Taurito

B. de Arguineguin

Presa de Chamoriscan

Los Palm Park

Puerto de Mogán

Tauro

LA PLAYA DE TAURO

Puerto Rico

Patalavaca

Cornisa

Las Casas

Arguineguin

Bahia de S.Agueda

PLAYA LA MELONER

LA VACA
LAS LAJAS
Punta del Roque
Punta de las Salinas
LA ISLETA
Punta del Camello
Bañaderos
La Isleta
Bahia del Confital
Puerto de la Luz
San Andrés
Cardones
Cambalud
Frontòn
Arucas
Las Palmas de Gran Canaria
Los Giles
Vegueta
Firgas
Moya
Tamaraceite
El Toscon
Tilos
El Palmar
San Lorenzo
Punta Casa Blanca
Monte Lentiscal
Tafira Baja
Teror
Tafira Alta
PLAYA DE LA LAJA
Punta del Palo
Valleseco
Mazagán
Sgdo. Corazón
Jinamar
Santa Brigída
La Atalaya
La Estrella
Valle de San Roque
Telde
PLAYA D. LA GARITA
Ariñez
La Gran Parada
San Mateo
La Garita
Las Lagunetas
Melenara
Valsequillo de G.C.
ElCaracol
Rincón
Nieves
949
La Colomba
Playa de Salinetas
Punta de Silva
La Breña
B. de Silva
Cuevas Blancas
Ruinas Históricas
Pasadilla
Rico Blanco
Arguatona
Punta de Gando
San Bartolome de Tirajana
Ingenio
Carrizal
Aeropuerto de Gando
Santa Lucia
Temisas
Agüimes
Teheral
912
PLAYA DEL BURRERO
Presa de Tirajana
Fataga
Presa de Fataga
B. de la Angostura
Mñ. de Arinaga
198
Punta de la Sal
Puercos
1001
Barranco de Tirajana
El Estanco
Arinaga
Punta del Mato
B. de Fataga
Sardina
Cruce de Sardina
Bahia de Arinaga
Aldea Blanca
Los Blancos
Vecindario
Canón del Aguila
Punta de Tenefe
Juan Grande
La Caleta
El Matorral
Barco Quebrado
PLAYA DEL CARDÓN
San Agustin
Berriel
PLAYA DE TARAJALILLO
Atlantic Ocean
PLAYA DEL INGLÉS
Maspalomas
Punta de Maspalomas

Las Palmas & The North

Gran Canaria is extraordinarily and naturally beautiful, but this beauty is not always instantly visible. The tourist may well feel distinctly un-seduced as the airport bus runs past barren landscapes dotted with cement plants and and necessary, but hardly picturesque, water purifying complexes towards Las Palmas de Gran Canaria; the road south of the airport to the resorts is no better, lined with skeletons of rudimentary plastic greenhouses. The grey colour of the houses is the result of a municipal tax: if you don't paint your house, you don't have to pay it.

But there is plenty to look forward to: as the bus rounds the corner after the dismal water-plant, Las Palmas de Gran Canaria stretches along the coast, basking like a lazy lizard in the sun. Down South, the bus rounds the bend to reveal miles of golden sands. This is what Gran Canaria is all about.

Gran Canaria's northern coast, with Las Palmas in the distance

This itinerary explores the area below San Telmo Park in Las Palmas, which is in two parts – the old town of Vegueta and Triana – separated by a wide highway, Juan de Quesada. Then further north, crossing the peninsula, to Mesa y Lopez, the main shopping street, and further north still to the port on the east side and Canteras Beach to the west.

–City bus No 1 leaves from near the Teatro Guiniguada at the bottom of Triana and runs almost the entire length of the peninsula. See map on page 22–

San Telmo Park, lit by attractive globular lamps, is the first place to learn about. It's in front of Estacio de Guaguas, the main bus station (the northbound number 1 stops right outside on Avenida Rafael Cabrera) and contains a pleasant church (much larger than it seems from outside); an early 19th century military building from which General Franco began to campaign to take over Spain in July 1936; a tourist information kiosk (rarely open); an irresistible Art Deco café (toilets in the basement); and the Hotel Parque whose second floor restaurant overlooks the square.

Heading down from San Telmo is **Calle Mayor de Triana**, a broad pedestrian walkway with plenty of seats and whose shops include a sedate, almost invisible McDonald's and a Marks & Spencers that only sells clothes. At roughly the middle, opposite Benetton, is the sleek **Koala Cafeteria** outside which on a Friday evening you might be lucky enough to catch a full orchestra playing, conductor in white tie and tails. Further down, the **Restaurant Triana** has outdoor seats and an extensive cafeteria menu.

Beside the BBV Bank, along Domingo J Navarro is **Fedac** (daily 9.30am–1pm, and Monday to Saturday 4–7pm), the government-sponsored Canarian handicrafts shop, choc-a-bloc with leather goods, baskets, lace cloths, tin kitchen utensils, carved wooden trunks, knives and pottery.

Where Triana meets Malteses is **Casa Ricardo**, the candy store of everybody's childhood dreams, one of a chain which offers jellied *cocodrilos*, *corazon de melocobon* (heart-shaped melon), grotesque *dentaduras foam* (teeth in blue, green and yellow) and European and American candy bars. Forty-five glass cartons offer many types of caramels and 28 varieties of raisins and nuts (including peanuts from the US and Brazil and six different sorts of almonds!). There's dried fruit in blocks and bags and a dozen different sticks of brightly coloured liquorice.

Head up Calle Cano to the right, where there's a saddle shop, some stylish art stores and the birthplace in 1843 of the

Casa de Colón

beloved Spanish novelist Benito Pérez Galdós who left home at 19 to study in Madrid, dying there in 1920 (see *Itinerary 6, page 45*). Back on Malteses, go left at Peregrina and opposite the pretty **Patio Peregrina** with its ivy-covered spiral staircase is **Atarecos**, whose name (explains its red-haired English-speaking owner Juana Suarez) means 'little old Canary things'. These include suede bags, local pottery and silver, stone *pintaderas* (the seals with which Guanches used to mark their possessions and sometimes themselves) and various other kinds of tasteful artwork.

Turn right at the wide street, in past times the frog-filled River Guiniguada, and walk through the **Plaza de las Ranas** (one lone marble *rana* – frog – sits beside the fountain) and into the **Plaza Calrasco**. The plaza is flanked at one side by the impressive Gabinete Literario, a private club, and at the other by a delightful café-filled indoor mall.

Down Malteses, of course, brings you back to the Mayor de Triana – the '*Ramblas*' – at the other side of which is the **Teatro Pérez Galdós**, its interior decorated by the internationally recognised artist Néstor Martin Fernández de la Torre (1887–1938) whose work can be seen in the Museo Néstor (see *Itinerary 6, page 46*). Outside stands a statue of Camille Saint-Saens who lived on the island at the turn of the 20th century. Behind the theatre is

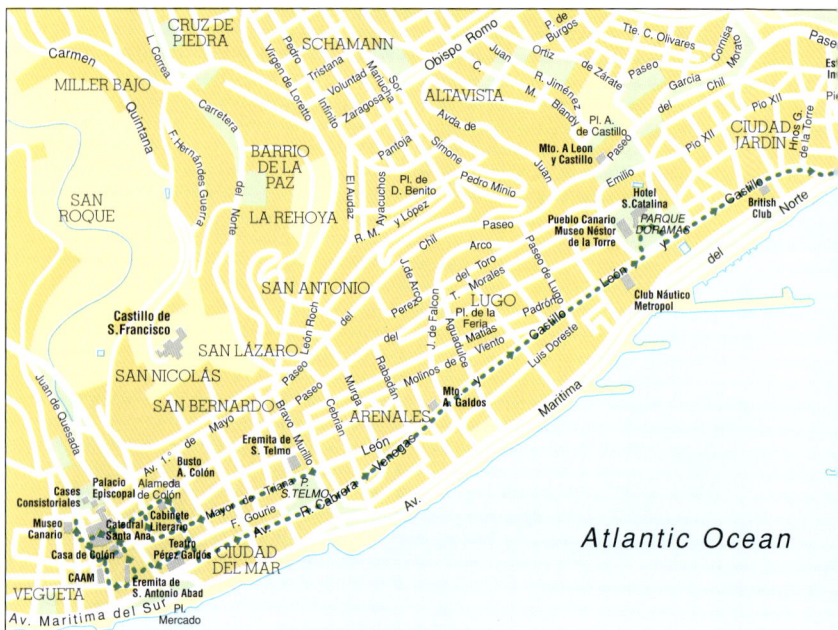

the 'around town' bus station from where the all-important number 1 bus leaves.

The busy highway beyond the theatre, Juan de Quesada, separates the Triana district from **Vegueta** where the city was founded by Juan Rejón in 1478. Vegueta is the loveliest part of town with its Andalusian-style balconies hanging over narrow cobbled streets.

Begin at the solidly-built **Mercado Las Palmas** and head up Calle Pelota past **Teatro Guiniguada** and behind the cathedral to the

On Plaza Santa Ana

Casa de Colón, much restored and rebuilt since it housed the island governor in the 15th century. It owes its fame to Christopher Columbus reputedly having stayed there in 1492 and contains a reconstruction of the poopdeck of *La Niña*, as well as models of this and its sister ships *La Pinta* and *Santa Maria* (see *Itinerary 6, page 44*).

Leaving the Casa de Colón, head along Calle Herrería, around the **Catedral Santa Ana** and into **Plaza Santa Ana**, with the town hall at one end and the bronze dogs – the *canes* who gave their name to the Canary Islands – at the other. Most tourists pose for photographs here. Entrance to the cathedral is via a door on Calle Espíritu Santo which is also the entrance to the **Museum of Religious Art** (see *Itinerary 6, page 44*), its Patio de los Naranjos lined with caged canaries – only one of which is yellow.

The cathedral, whose mixed styles reflect its construction through four centuries, has numerous chapels, in one of which lies the embalmed body in a glass case of Bishop Codina

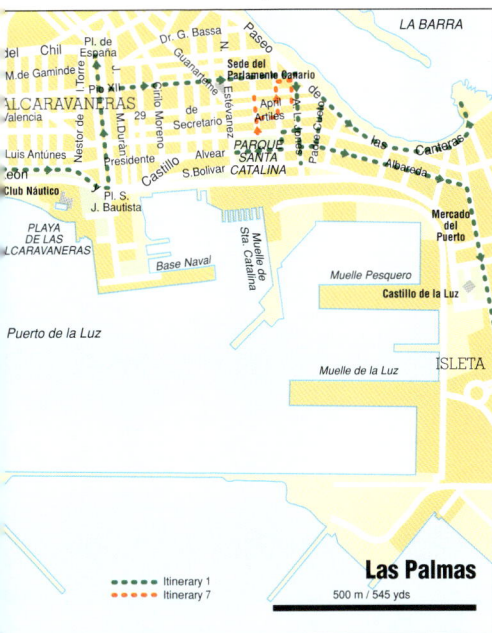

Las Palmas

500 m / 545 yds

••••• Itinerary 1
••••• Itinerary 7

(died 1857), a possible candidate for canonisation for his sterling work during a cholera epidemic early in the 19th century. Glorious rainbow shadows are projected onto the pillars from the sun shining through stained glass windows.

On Las Palmas' most photographed street, the **Calle de los Balcones**, is CAAM (Centro Atlantico de Arte Moderno) in a much-admired five-storey building by Sáenz de Oíza which, despite its 18th-century facade, is as modern as its collection (see *Itinerary 6, page 45*). Nearby is **El Museo Canario** (see *page 46*) on Calle Dr Chil, named after the anthropologist who founded it more than a century ago. Here you can see dioramas of Guanche cave life along with such utensils as pestles and mortars. There is also a reproduction of the Painted Cave at Galdár, which has been closed for restoration work for some years.

Pérez Galdós in stone

Back down the cobbled pedestrian precinct of Balcones, past a vintage barber shop on the corner and through the narrow alleyway, Calle Algaba, to the shrine/chapel of **San Antonio Abad** where Columbus reputedly heard mass before continuing his voyage to 'discover' America.

If you're ready for lunch, head down Audienca behind the chapel to Calle Augustin Millares where the attractive **Trattoria La Dolce Vita** is open 1.30–4pm and 9pm–12.30am. Alternatively, turn along Mendizabal at the bottom of the street and head left to **El Herreño** or its eponymous snack-bar across the street.

Walk back up the '*Ramblas*' or take the number1 bus (which makes a stop at the far side of San Telmo Park). The bus heads up

San Antonio Abad

Venegas behind the multiplex cinema (Multi Scenes Royal, on Leon y Castillo, a few blocks above the square), running into Leon y Castillo at Plaza de la Feria, a soulless square with an ugly statue of Benito Pérez Galdós. You'll want to alight at the **Hotel Santa Catalina** to stroll through its lush, semi-tropical grounds to the enclosed plaza which adjoins the Canarian Village (see below) and contains a tourist office (seldom open), some handicraft shops, the expensive Restaurant Bodegon and the wonderful **Museo Néstor** (Parque Doramas, tel: 24 51 35; Tuesday to Friday 10am–1pm and 4–8pm, Sunday 11am–midday)

The museum occupies a well-lit, two-storey space with antique bookcases; a dress from a 1934 production of *Cavalleria Rusticana* for which Néstor did the sets; his sketches for the Pérez Galdós theatre; and numerous paintings and posters from his relatively short life. Néstor, who had studios in Madrid and Paris, designed the adjoining **Pueblo Canaria** (Canarian Village), which was built after his death in 1938 by his brother Miguel. Music and dancing is presented here on Thursdays at 5.30pm and Sundays at 11.45am by Canarians in traditional costume.

Santa Catalina Hotel is the favourite of most celebs who visit Las Palmas, an olde worlde sort of place filled with every modern luxury except shops (not even a news-stand). There's a nighttime casino and a lobby with slot machines that are open when the casino isn't. At the rear is the sandy **Parque Doramas**, named for one of the last native chiefs to resist the Spanish invaders, who in 1491 was killed by the lance of the coloniser Pedro de Vera .

Kiosk on San Telmo Park

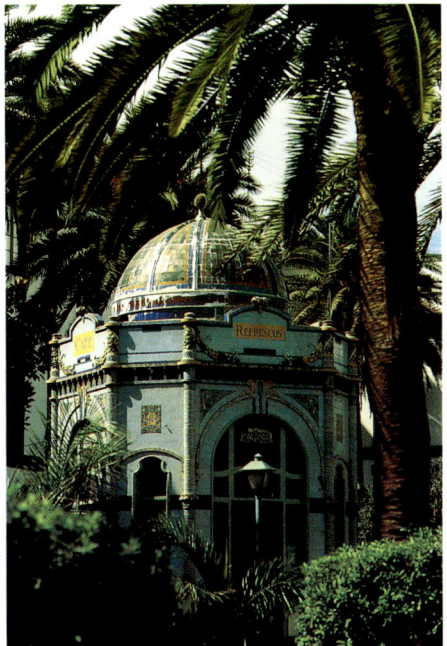

The number 1 bus, still heading up towards the port, passes the Club Nautico and at the broad Mesa y Lopez turns inland, stopping behind **Corte del Ingles**, the Spanish department store that now occupies both sides of the main street, having absorbed its major competitor. A world-class store, Corte del Ingles has pretty much everything, including an extravagantly well-stocked super- market in the basement and reasonably priced cafés on the upper floors of both branches. Mesa y Lopez, which ends in the **Plaza de Espagña** with its outdoor cafés, is one of the best shopping streets in Las Palmas.

Dancer at the Pueblo Canario

Continuing northward, bus number 1 heads up the dozen blocks of Tomas Miller to about the midway point of Las Canteras beach, passing **La Strada** restaurant (the all-you-can-eat buffet costs about £5) before turning inland again along Alfredo Jones, one block above the **Parque Santa Catalina** (not to be confused with the Hotel Santa Catalina, a mile to the south). In the park here, scene of the annual Las Palmas festival, is the main tourist office (Alfonso Falcon is multilingual); the main post office; cafés and – a block away – the towering **Hotel Sol Bardinos** whose 24th floor café is inexpensive and offers a view of the port rivalled only by its 26th floor swimming pool.

Here at Santa Catalina park you are at the beginning of the peninsula's narrowest point, an area flanked by the **Playa de Las Canteras** at one side and the port at the other and served by the number 1 bus which turns past the covered market and the 15th century **Castillo de la Luz** (closed to the public) to terminate at another bus station on Calle Juan Rejon. The narrow streets north of the park – Luis Morote, 29 de Abril, Sacasta – are filled with Indian and other ethnic restaurants, electronics stores and a sex shop or two. At night this area is the nearest Las Palmas has to a red light district.

On the beach side, the promenade sports one restaurant after another, all with outdoor tables and multilingual menus. **Al Macaroni's** is good value with its courteous old-time waiter of the type you don't see much any more, and **Roma**, near the top of the beach, is as good if not better. It's a pleasant walk which is best concluded, especially in the evening, at **Puntija Plaza**, the café underneath the **Punto del Recife**, a wide stone jetty that marks the end of the beach. From the windy terrace here where, strangely, few tourists are seen, you can sit and survey the entire 3-km (2-mile) sweep of the Bay of Canteras.

The hotels fronting the bay are predictably luxurious, with comfortable lounges: the Meliá and the Reina Elizabeth, with its rooftop café beside the pool, are especially pleasant resting places. But in the surrounding streets, near the Reina particularly, are several cheaper hotels. Check also along Juan Rejon and neighbouring streets such as Princessa (see *Accommodation, page 79*).

Las Canteras beach

26

2. To the Finger of God

Via Guía and Gáldar to Reptilandia and the Dedo de Dios (God's Finger). Return via the Valle de Agaete. With stops en route, this itinerary is about a 6-hour drive. Remember that you will be changing altitude – Los Berrazales is 400m (1,312ft). Puerto de las Nieves is a pebble beach so take appropriate footwear.

–Bus number 103 runs from Las Palmas to Puerto de las Nieves via San Andrés, Guía, Gáldar and Agaete every hour from 8am–10pm. By car you can also take in Reptilandia, Cuevas de las Cruces and Los Berrazales to which buses do not run. Cenobio de Valerón is a couple of hundred yards off the highway near the road to Moya.–

The highway hugs the coast for the early part of the route and on stormy days the sea along the storm-lashed northern shore is white for hundreds of yards out. The startling **Auditorio Alfredo Kraus**, looking improbably like a modern version of an ancient fortress, is the last landmark on the city's outskirts.

If you are driving, follow the signposts for Agaete. At the city's end, you will see the road to the north (Norte) clearly signposted. Just before the spectacular soaring bridge of Puente de Silva is a turning off to the left which you reach via a roundabout. If you have come by bus, get off here and walk.

The road winds up to the **Cenobio de Valerón** (signposted) one of the few archaeological sites open (in part) to the public but ever more in danger of being closed. The rockface is honeycombed with scores of caves hollowed from the soft volcanic rock, which for years were thought to be a convent but which are now believed to have been a granary. Nearly 200 steps lead up to the misnamed

The North

cenobio ('convent'), but the entrance is barred because of the danger of rock falls. Remains of stone benches on the hill above identify the site as a *tagoror*, a Guanche place of assembly.

Looking out from this viewpoint, you can see the high rock from which it is alleged the last *guanarteme*, Bentejuí, threw himself. (See *History and Culture* section, page 12). The Puente de Silva is bedecked with wire netting to prevent contemporary Canary islanders from attempting to emulate him.

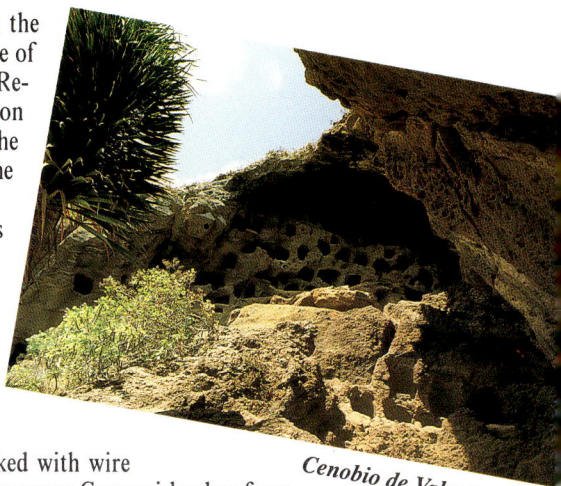

Cenobio de Valerón

Back in your vehicle on the C-810, you will soon pass through a series of tunnels, after which you will notice banana plantations on both sides of the road, signifying that you are now passing though the island's main banana-growing area.

You will now pass through the two rival towns of **Guía,** famous for its rennet cheese (*queso flor de Guía*) and **Gáldar**, the pre-Spanish capital of Gran Canaria. Gáldar's famous Guanche site, the **Cueva Pintada** or 'Painted Cave', has been closed for restorations that have already lasted four years and through the locked gate the site looks like a garbage dump. The street to go up is Audienca past the tiny Plaza de Cristo before reaching the centre of town.

Local crop

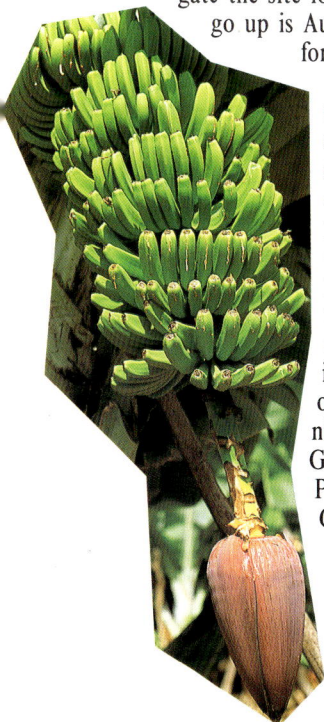

The virgin Andamana, who had a reputation for being 'a mediator of great wisdom', lived in the Painted Cave which actually comprises a series of seven caves, each with pits on the floor and traces of painting. The largest cave is about 5m (16½ft) wide and 3m (10ft) high with a frieze near the top of the walls containing triangles, chevrons, squares and concentric circles of black, red and white. It is the only such place on the islands decorated with colour Some of the pre-colonial relics from the cave are on show in Gáldar's Town Hall, and a replica of the Painted Cave can be viewed in the Museo Canario in Las Palmas.

Gáldar is sometimes wistfully referred to by its ancient name, *Ciudad de los Guanartemes* – 'City of the Rulers' – the rulers

Cave house, Sardina del Norte

referring to Tenesor Semidan and his Guanche predecessors. They had governed the island from a palace believed to have occupied the site on which the 19th century Santiago de los Caballeros church now stands. The inner courtyard of the **Town Hall**, at one corner of the square, houses a gigantic 280-year-old dragon tree. This species was held in reverence by the Guanches, who conducted religious rites in its hollow trunk. It has become the symbol of the Canary Islands.

A dragon tree looks more like a lily than a tree, its 'trunk' formed by the interwining of many branches around a space in the middle. Both the trunk and branches are smooth and bare, carrying no foliage except short, spear-like leaves at the tips. Thus the tree resembles a giant mushroom. When cut, a thick, blood red substance oozes out, a red resin held by Greeks, Romans and Arabs to have medicinal properties and also used in dyes until the arrival of synthetics.

Just beyond Gáldar, you can drive along a road that forks to the west, towards **Sardina del Norte**. This small fishing village has a charming beach that's great for swimming and snorkelling.

Back at the crossroads with Hoya de Pineda, you will see the signpost for **Reptilandia** (Monday to Sunday 11am–5.30pm), a reptile park run by a British couple and their Canary partner. Here you can see chameleons, giant tortoises and crocodiles in open enclosures resembling their natural habitat. The monkeys, tarantulas, poisonous toads, snakes, and the latest acquisition, the hissing cockroaches, are all either in cages or in glass cases.

Continuing on the C-810, the road winds down past the **Cuevas de las Cruces**, a system of caves on the left-hand side of the road. Continue to Agaete, a pleasant whitewashed town of narrow streets which sits at the foot of a fertile *barranco* replete with mangoes, papaya, dates and avocados. The **Huerto de las Flores**, an enclosed garden

Reptilandia

that was a favourite of the poet Tomás Morales (see *Itinerary 4*) is open weekday mornings. It is better to stay on the bus, however, and continue a mile further to **Puerto de las Nieves**, a fishing village whose tiny chapel is the scene of an August festival called the 'Procession of the Branches' – referring to the pagan custom of bearing *rama* (branches) from the mountains to the seashore to whip the waves bringing rain.

Along Avenida Las Poetas is the seaside theatre (made of straw) in which painter/violinist Pedro Matthias Kraus presents his *Teatro de Marionetas*, a Saturday evening puppet show with extra performances by special request (tel: 939 229 414).

The port is crowded at weekends, explaining the apparently disproportionate number of restaurants. First-time visitors always head for **El Dedo de Dios**, an airy eating place with floor-to-ceiling windows looking out over the cove in which a monolith of stone stands in the shape of a fist with its index finger sticking up. The restaurant is named after this landmark's epithet, meaning 'the finger of God'. After lunch, pay a visit to the **Ermita de las Nieves**, which contains a magnificent 16th-century Flemish triptych that has recently been restored.

El Dedo de Dios (God's Finger)

If driving, take the road to the east signposted **El Valle**. The road gradually winds its way up through this incredibly beautiful valley, past La Casa Romántica and the hotel at **Los Berrazales**. Be warned: the bend just before the hotel, immediately after the water bottling factory, is particularly dangerous, especially if you meet the local bus coming the other way, so take care. There used to be a spa at Los Berrazales; this no longer exists but the exhilarating view down the valley is an experience in itself.

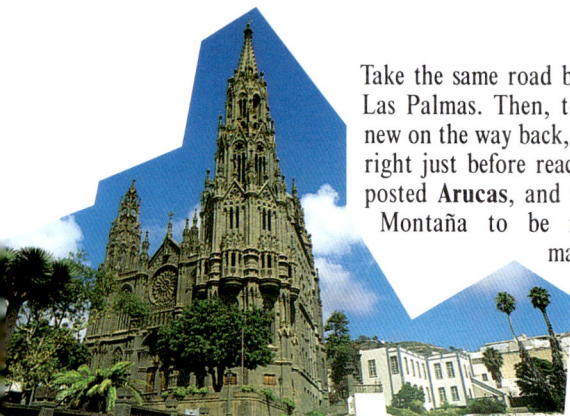

Take the same road back down and towards Las Palmas. Then, to introduce something new on the way back, take the road off to the right just before reaching Baña-deros, signposted **Arucas**, and twist your way up the Montaña to be rewarded by another magnificent view over the neo-Gothic church of **San Juan Bautista** (sometimes wrongly referred to by the locals as 'the Cathedral' on account of its size) and over the bay of Las

The neo-Gothic San Juan Bautista

Palmas. There is a restaurant on the top of the hill, so you can sip a Tia Maria liqueur whilst enjoying the view.

Locals sometimes claim that the church was designed by Gaudi, but it is almost certainly just in the style of the famous Barcelona architect. The distinctive stone of its construction, however, is of a local type and was also used to build a tower in the nearby **Jardín de la Marquesa**, a botanical preserve that was presented to the city by the marquesa whose mansion sits at one end of it. Including a banana plantation and dragon trees, there are more than 2,000 species from as far afield as Malaya, Australia and Mexico in the garden, which is a favourite with tour groups and has a bar and restaurant.

Arehucas rum, produced from the sugar cane fields around Arucas, is made at a local distillery which can be visited by arrangement. Rich volcanic soils, year-round mild temperatures and varied elevations result in crops of bananas, oranges, coffee, dates, suga cane, tobacco, tomatoes, potatoes, grapes, flowers and some cereals. In the 19th century cochineal was produced locally, but the emergence of synthetic dyes ended this industry.

The celebrated Guanche hero Doramas was killed by Spanish invaders in 1481 at the Montana de Aruca outside town, whereupon his followers are said to have thrown themselves into the ravine in despair.

When hunger strikes

If you are driving back to Las Palmas via the main road (c-810), you may want to stop off at Las Arenas, a big shopping complex, to see what the locals eat (at the best prices in town) in Continente – and if you are craving a Big Mac, this is the place to find one.

3. To the Top of the Island

This six-hour itinerary goes via the Jardín Canario up to the Pinar de Tamadaba (which lies 1,444m/4,737ft above sea level so take some warm clothing in case you get cold). It offers spectacular views all the way along a route that takes in La Atalaya, San Mateo and Artenara.

–From the flyover at the Pérez Galdós theatre, take the c-811 to Tafira. Alternatively, buses 311 and 312 run from Las Palmas to Bandama, from where a taxi may be necessary to view the caldera; buses 301/302/303 go to San Mateo; bus number 305 goes to Tejeda. All pass the Jardín Canario and go via Santa Brigida. See map on page 28.–

A visit by bus to the attractive **Jardín Canario** is the shortest trip you can make out of town – many buses pass – but unfortunately it is difficult to get back. The bus drops you off for a short walk downhill to the excellent restaurant/bar at the top, but if you descend the hundreds of feet into the garden itself there is no bus along the bottom road. And having climbed back up again you will discover that the nearest bus stop for the return journey to Las Palmas is in Tafira, half a mile uphill on a main road with a very narrow pavement for much of the way.

The garden is laid out so that you can observe most of it from the bust of Viera y Clavijo (1713–1813), the park's founder, where a map locates everything from the twin dragon trees and volcanic cave to the waterlily pond and cactus grove. A path along the edge of the cliff to your right leads to the windy archway.

The highway continues up through the narrow part of Tafira, with signs indicating the golf course of Bandama, which is perched on top of the volcanic crater of the same name. The **Caldera de Bandama**, whose diameter is 1,000m (3,300ft), is 630ft (200m) deep with a solitary farm at the bottom. The farmer has become accustomed to taking time off from tending his chickens and goats to answer questions from curious tourists who make the 30-minute descent. On the way down are some of the earliest Guanche cave dwellings. The best viewpoint, offering sweeping views of much of the island, is where the road ends at the Pico de Bandama. There's a small cafe at this endpoint.

The **Golf Club of Bandama** was founded by the British community, which still tends to centre around Tafira, possibly because the climate here

Beware of pedestrians on the Tafira road

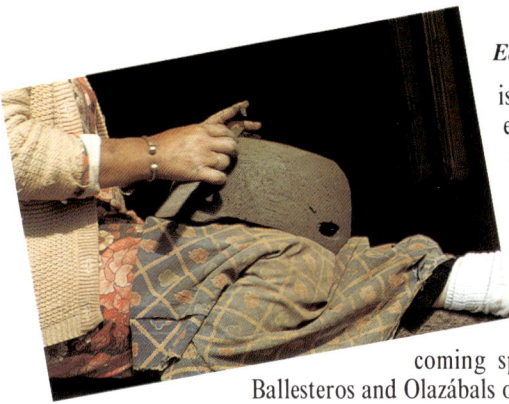

Earthenware

is cooler and wetter than elsewhere on the island and therefore more reminiscent of home. This is the oldest golf club in Spain (set up in 1891) and its nine holes are very carefully tended. Golf is now an up-and-coming sport in Spain, with the Ballesteros and Olazábals of the world blazing trails of glory. The Caldera is also a favourite haunt of local courting couples (also, perhaps, because it is cooler); watch out for oddly parked cars.

A road runs along the side of the golf course, past the British School and the riding school to the cave village of **La Atalaya**, famous for its earthenware pottery, which is hand-moulded and left to bake in the sun. The most famous of the potters, Panchito, died a few years ago but his disciples make sure that his memory lives on in their splendid artworks. To enter the village turn right at the crossroads and then up to the left; the best views and best pottery are to be found down a flight of steps behind the village square where the church stands.

Once back in the car, and if you are feeling adventurous, follow the narrow road up behind the church. A very rudimentary traffic light, which works highly efficiently nonetheless, controls the traffic up to **La Concepción**, one of the most exclusive residential sites on the island thanks to its magnificent views. The little shrine on the left, now almost abandoned to its fate, is the oldest *ermita* on the island.

Back down the slope and turn down to the left beside the church square. Another turn left will take you down the Carretera de la Atalaya

Roads here are narrow and twisting

to the main road. Turn left at the crossroads but be careful because visibility to the right is very poor. You will now pass through **Santa Brígida** where Dutch invaders, under Van der Hoes, were driven back and out of Gran Canaria by the islanders in 1599. Con-

34

tinue on the C-811, running past Pino Santo on the right and the old British country club, now turned into a restaurant called Monte Verde, on your left.

A little farther up the road, also on the left, in El Madroñal, you will see the restaurant **Martel** (open every day). The owner of this typical Canary restaurant also has one of the best wine-cellars on the island and offers a wide variety of cheeses and olives in *mojo* (a delicious herb sauce).

Back in the car, continue up the road to **San Mateo** where, shortly after an incongruously ugly statue presumably representing the noble peasant, on the right, you will see the ethnological museum of **Cho Zacarías** (Monday to Saturday, mornings only; closed Sunday). This is well worth an unhurried visit; if there are coaches parked outside, it is best to take a stroll round the village first, calling in at the **Pastelería San Mateo**, just a little farther up the pavement, where you will be able to buy the delicious *bien-mesabe*, a sticky honey and almond confection. The local market, also worth a look inside, is along the first road on your left.

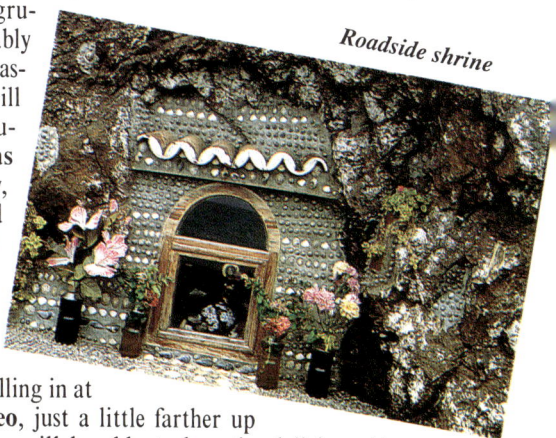

Roadside shrine

Your best option for lunch is the restaurant in Cho Zacarías (closed Monday). The restaurant is decorated with exhibits, including typical farming implements and an enormous bellows beside the fireplace. The food is always delicious and the owner, who speaks both English and German, will be pleased to recommend dishes.

It is a winding, hair-raising drive up through the mountains (there is a particularly nasty bend at La Lechuza) to the solitary *parador* on Gran Canaria at tiny **Cruz de Tejeda**, 35km (22 miles) southwest of Las Palmas and 1,830m (6,000ft) up in the mountains. Nevertheless, you will be treated to stupendous views most of the way ('petrified storm' is how the renowned Canarian poet Unamuno described the scenery). The comfortable hotel, designed by Néstor de la Torre, is one of the famous state-owned chain known for comfort, luxuriance, good food and magnificent surroundings. Beside the bus stop (last bus back to Las Palmas 5.30pm) are souvenir stalls, donkey rides and a café.

A trio of outstanding volcanic pillars – **Roque Nublo, Roque Bentaiga** and **El Fraile** – are clearly visible, 4,877-m (16,000ft) high Nublo offering a mountainous track for ambitious climbers from the village of **Ayacata**, northwest of San Bartolome.

The road from Tejeda winds ever higher, all the way to the **Pico de las Nieves** – 'peak of the snows' – at 1,949m (6,395 ft), where a truck offering drinks and sandwiches sits below the military communications tower. There's a semi-panoramic view with small communities in the distance and clouds lingering in hollows to the west. (To get taxi here from Maspolomas costs about $50 plus waiting time).

If you are driving, return to the C-811, and go back to a fork signposted for **Artenara** (see *Itinerary 4*). The road to Artenara winds around gorges and terraced landscapes but affords wonderful views. The village itself is tiny. Just before the village square, down to the right, look for a signpost for **La Silla**. This restaurant is entered via a tunnel, at the end of which you will be welcomed by the most spectacular view, weather permitting, of Roque Nublo and Roque Bentaiga. This restaurant is well worth visiting on its own (anyone who has not stayed the pace should not despair since it is included in another itinerary in this book). For those who want to experience life as a cave-dweller, several caves have been converted into accommodation as part of a programme for rural tourism.

The same road gradually winds its way up to the dizzy heights of the **Pinar de Tamadaba**, 1,444m (4,737ft). This spectacular pine forest offers fabulous views over Agaete and even as far as Fuji-shaped Mount Teide on Tenerife, which at 3,719m/11,900ft is Spain's highest mountain.

The highway to **Teror** spirals around curves so acute that bus drivers constantly sounds their horns. The mountain bus ride is through a picturesque landscape of white houses perched on precipitous hillsides and shades of green from the algae-covered lakes to the darker hues of moss, trees and cacti. A grove of baby pine trees can be seen at the road side at Tamaraceite, a Guanche word that means just that, before you descend into what is probably Gran Canaria's prettiest town, Teror (population 11,200).

The 18th century **basilica** contains a jewel-bedecked statue of the **Virgen del Pino**, the island's patron saint, a vision of whom is said to have appeared in a treetop on September 8, 1481. On this

Typical balcony in Teror

View of Bentaiga

day each year (see *Calendar of Special Events, page 73*) people from all over the islands set off in groups to walk, or even crawl on their knees, along the road to the shrine.

The plaza in front of the church is for pedestrians only and is usually thronged with tourists (especially for the Sunday morning market) who patronise the shops selling lace and souvenirs and visit the fascinating **Casa Museo de los Patrones de la Virgen**. The furnished rooms in this 17th-century house (built around a delightful patio) look as though they have been frozen in time. Also on show here are paintings by Georg Heydrick, a Polish-born artist who has been running a studio/gallery a few doors away for many years. Knowledgeable and multilingual, he is the creator of an unusually descriptive map of the island.

The adjoining plaza is named for a former resident, Teresa de Bolívar, first wife of Simon Bolívar the 19th-century liberator of South America. Down on the spacious lower terrace, facing the grassy hills, are a couple of open-air cafés.

The road from Teror back to Las Palmas is fairly fast at first, but after **Tenoya** it becomes narrow and winding. It then passes through Tamaraceite and back into **Las Palmas** via the Feria del Atlántico. If you look up to the left, at the second traffic lights, you will see the Feria: the Trade Fair precinct where the fair takes place annually in April. From here, continue straight down the hill, keeping in the left-hand lane, round the back of the football stadium and straight down to the Plaza de España. Here, turn second right off the roundabout and down Mesa y López, past the department stores Galerías Preciados. Follow this street as far as it goes and, at the end, turn left for the Parque Santa Catalina.

Teror's Virgen del Pino

Reward yourself at the end of this long day with a drink on the terrace of the **Hotel Meliá** on the Paseo de las Canteras (bearing east), followed by dinner in this hotel's beautifully decorated restaurant **El Jardín Botanico**, with its magnificent views over the beach. If you are not too tired after dinner, make for **Pachá**, a disco (Calle Simón Bolívar) along from the Elder and Miller buildings on Parque Santa Catalina. Alternatively, enjoy the balmy night with a last drink on a terrace bar in the park itself.

4. Moya, Fontanales and Artenara

A morning excursion into the interior via Moya, incorporating the museum of an island poet, pine and laurel forests and a holy shrine. Especially recommended for those who missed out Artenara on Itinerary 3. A jeep is essential for the stretch which takes you through the Tilos de Moya to Fontanales.

–From Las Palmas bus 116 runs through Cabo Verde to Moya, and 2–3 times a day bus 110 runs between Moya and Galdar. Three times a day bus 118 runs between Arucas and Fortanales via Moya. From Las Palmas, bus 220 runs to Artenara via Teror three times a day. See map on p. 28.–

Follow the signposts out of Las Palmas towards Agaete. The road runs along the coast but is marred by haphazard building work (islanders leave their properties unpainted in order to avoid the hefty taxes levied on finished buildings). Run through **Bañaderos** and take the turning off to the right, signposted **Pagador**. Turn inland after San Andres from the north coast road. It's a long, steep climb up to **Moya** whose immense church, Nuestra Señora de la Candelaria, is perched on the edge of a ravine (two earlier versions collapsed into it). At a safe distance away, the **birthplace of Tomás Morales** (1885–1921), the revered Canarian poet, is preserved as an attractive museum. The lovely house contains first editions of his writings and the walls are covered with blow-ups of his poems.

Grand Canary Harbour on the booming Atlantic
With its red lamps in the warm night's haze,
And the moon's disc beneath the blue romantic
Depth, gleaming in shifting serenity of seaways

Fresh flowers adorn the tables and flowers and trees line a whitewashed patio.

Morales studied medicine in Madrid but afterwards became a lyric poet. Returning in 1909 to the Canaries, where he won first prize in a poetry contest judged by the eminent Miguel de Unamuno, he wrote plays and newspaper articles, married and settled in Agaete where he died aged 37.

The easy drive up to Fontanales is via the left turn at the crossroads (note the signpost). Otherwise, and only if you are driving a jeep because the going is tough, continue straight on and take the next turning off to the left where **Los Tilos de Moya** is signposted. Much of this laurel forest has been closed to the public in an effort to

Moya

Moya street

halt environmental damage. The road (always open) is not often used and you can tell why; proceed slowly as it is narrow as well as winding and cars may come down in the opposite direction, often on a steep incline. However, the countryside is beautiful and the sense of travelling through parts of the island that even the natives do not know is exhilarating.

Fontanales is a typical Canary village nestling in a valley between volcanic hills. If you have come via Los Tilos, you turn left at the main road and enter Fontanales the back way, past the church. Otherwise, you come in on the main road. Park near **Restaurante Sibora** or **Bar Fontanales**, good places for a drink and *tapas* (animal lovers be warned: the walls of the Bar Fontanales are adorned with hunting trophies).

Back on the road, on the right-hand side about 1km (½ mile) further on, is **El Cortijo**, an example of the development of rural tourism on Gran Canaria. As well as offering comfortable accommodation, on sale there are local delicacies and wines.

Regaining the main road, follow signposts to **Artenara**. Here, stop off to have lunch in the **Mesón de la Silla**, which besides serving good and reasonably-priced food in pleasant surroundings offers anyone who didn't follow Itinerary 3 the opportunity to photograph the peaks of **Roque Nublo** and **Roque Bentaiga** from the verandah. Artenara itself is little more than a square but a narrow road running beside the church (best travelled on foot) leads to the quaint grotto of the **Virgen de la Cuevita**, the site of a procession in August (see *Calendar of Special Events, page 73*).

Suitably refreshed, you can either drive back to Las Palmas, taking the C-811 via **San Mateo** and **Santa Brígida** (as *Itinerary 3*), or, if you have time to spare (about half an hour each way) and have not taken this route before, continue to the **Pinar de Tamadaba** (also described in *Itinerary 3*). Whichever of these routes you choose, you could return via **Hoya de Pineda** (slightly farther along the road from Artenara in the direction of Tamadaba), **Montaña Vergara**, back down past the Cenobio de Valerón (see *Itinerary 2*) and on to the main road back to Las Palmas via Bañaderos. This option is hair-raising at times but the magnificent views more than make up for that.

5. Barranco de Guayadeque

A half-day excursion to the deep ravine (Barranco) of Guayadeque via the windswept regions of Telde and Ingenio. Lunch in a cave restaurant in the Barranco where, on Sunday, holidays and at other busy times, you can sample 'sancocho', a special fish dish.

—Drivers should take the motorway down to the South (GC-1); jeep advisable. From Las Palmas, bus number 12 runs to Telde via Marzagan; bus 11 runs to Agüimes via Ingenio. There is no bus service to the Barranco de Guayadeque. See map on page 42.—

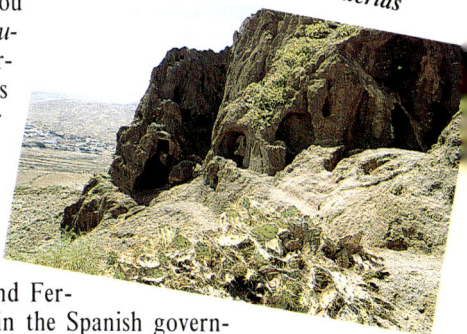
Caves at Cuatro Puertas

Leave **Las Palmas** by the road for the airport and turn off where you see Telde signposted. **Telde**, *la ciudad de los muebles* (the city of furniture), has more furniture shops per square metre than any other town on the islands. Telde (population 82,000) is Gran Canaria's second largest town. It is the birthplace of the celebrated León y Castillo brothers: Juan, who built the port of Las Palmas; and Fernando, who became a minister in the Spanish government. Their home on the eponymously named street in Telde has been turned into a museum. The town is also famous for its faith-healers, its superstitions and the fact that its inhabitants have won the Christmas national lottery prize (known as *El Gordo* or the fatty) more often than anywhere else in Spain.

Entering town the bus passes a remarkable, modernist fountain resembling a space ship with sheets of water for windows. The *bar-*

Looking down the Barranco

rio San Francisco and adjoining San Juan, where part of the **Basilica San Juan** dates back to the 16th century, are the prettiest parts of town. Inside, as in other churches these days, visitors who want to light a candle for their loved ones can drop a coin in a slot which illuminates an electric lamp. The church contains a valuable Flemish altarpiece and a curious lightweight sculpture of Christ made in Mexico from maize.

A street close to the church is called Commandante Franco and another has been named for the poet Pablo Neruda, Franco's ideological enemy. On Conde de la Vega Grande, named for the count who was instrumental in developing the tourist industry in the south of the island, orange-bearing trees line the pavements. Ancient wooden balconies overhang cobbled streets and a small tropical garden adjoins a children's playground and a menagerie of singing and chirping birds (cockatiels, parakeets, parrots and peacocks).

In ancient times Telde was the base for the *guanarteme*, the ruler of the southern part of the island, the other ruler being in Galdár. Together with Gáldar, Telde was thus the main centre for the original Guanches and it was the site of the discovery of the emblematic *ídolo de Tara*, one of their cherished idols. A sign in front of the Basilica San Juan claims this was 'a privileged place where the most noble houses were situated. They were the homes of the Andalucian knights'. A 16th- century report to the king of Spain from the military engineer Leonardo Torriani indicated that 14,000 Guanche dwellings had been found in the area, many of

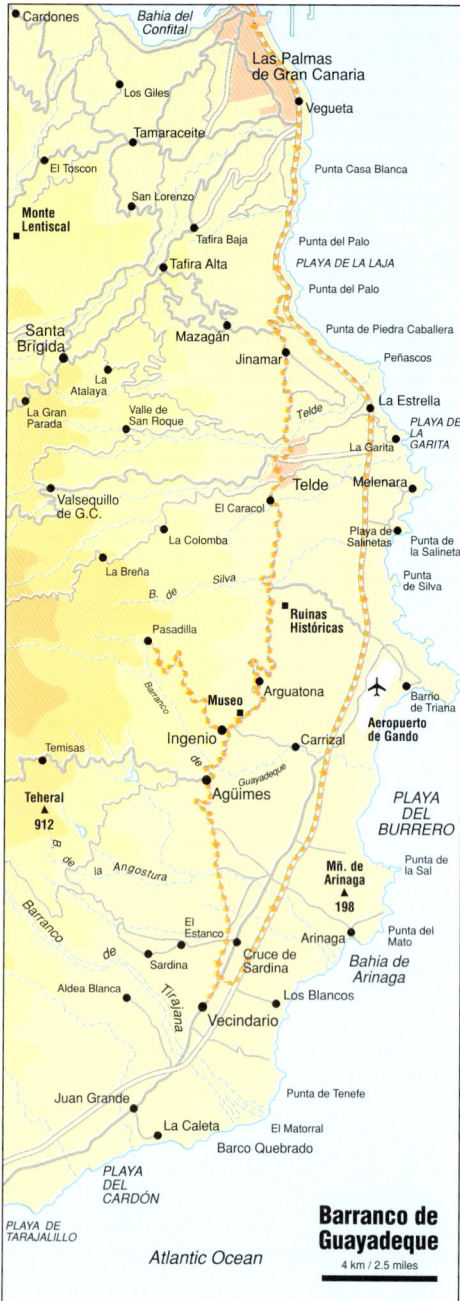

Lacemaker in El Museo de Piedras

them in the nearby *barranco*.

Many caves can still be seen on the **Montaña de las Cuatro Puertas**, believed to have been a sacred Guanche gathering place, on the Ingenio road to the south of town. The Guanches worshipped *Acorán* (the Greatest or Highest) to whom animal sacrifices were made at cave sanctuaries or sacred mountains such as the 1,404m (4,607ft) Roque Bentaiga, whose immense square shape dominates the Parralillo reservoir near the centre of the island.

Continue down the C-812 past **Aguatona** towards Ingenio, named after the Portuguese for sugar-mill. This region was famous for its sugar-cane production, although it is much diminished nowadays. Just outside Ingenio, you should not miss **El Museo de Piedras** (daily 9am–6pm) which has a fascinating display of old farm tools and, as the name suggests, rocks.

Back in the car, continue into **Ingenio**. At the crossroads, on the corner, you may see the locals selling *morenas*, big electric eels which are considered a great delicacy. It is worth turning right, where the Barranco de Guayadeque is signposted, then right again and into the town square. Ingenio was a town largely founded by the Portuguese and has inherited a tradition of witchcraft and superstition from the large slave population which inhabited it for a long time. The glorious **Barranco de Guadayeque**, once an ancient river bed stretching from the mountains to the sea, is defined by immense cliffs at each side, all green with shrubs, cactus and occasional homes with solar water collectors.

Continue along the road to the right, winding up to the restaurant, housed in a maze of caves and offering another breathtaking view down the gully. Here you can eat typical Canary food. On Sunday and holidays the restaurant serves *sancocho* (salted fish served with sweet potatoes and *mojo* and accompanied by *gofio* kneaded with milk and bananas); it is the only restaurant still to serve it.

From the Barranco, wend your way down to **Agüimes**, whose carnival celebrations are said to beat any on the islands, down through **Vecindario** which is called *la ciudad de los Mer-*

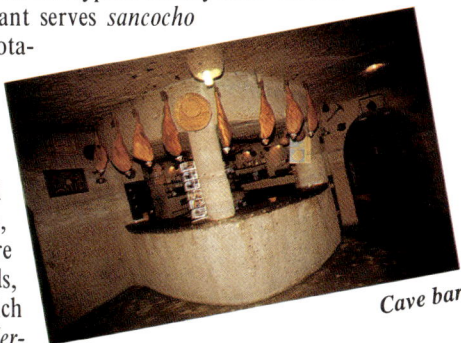

Cave bar

cedes on account of the many rich people who live there. Regain the main road back to Las Palmas, leaving behind the beaches of **Melenara**, **Playa del Hombre** and **La Garita**, small, badly maintained beaches which do not merit a stop-off unless you are hot and dusty.

Guanche mummy remains in the Museo Canario

6. Las Palmas: Museums and Galleries

Many visitors to Gran Canaria spend most of their time on the beach, visiting Las Palmas only for shopping. But there are many interesting museums to see, some of which are on Itinerary 1. Parking can be a big problem in Vegueta, so walk or take taxis.

The most interesting museum is undoubtedly **El Museo Canario**, Calle Dr. Chil 25, tel: 31 56 00 (weekdays 10am–8pm, weekends 10am–2pm). The famous Guanche mummies, not too well preserved, are on display in glass cases upstairs along with row after row of unadorned Cro Magnon skulls and *pintaderas*, the terracotta stamps with which Guanche adorned their property or themselves.

A little farther up Calle Dr Chil, on the right-hand side, is the **Square of Santo Domingo**. It was here that the Guanches formally submitted to the Spanish invaders in the presence of the famous Banner of the Conquest (now in the Catedral Santa Ana). Walk back down the far side of the church on the square, across Plaza Santa Ana and past the Episcopal Palace (undergoing restoration) across from the Cathedral. Cross at the traffic lights.

Behind the Cathedral is the **Museum of Religious Art**, Espíritu Santo 20, tel: 31 49 89 (weekdays 9am–1.30pm and 4–6.30pm, Saturday 9am–2pm). Half a dozen rooms contain portraits and religious artifacts; the pinewood and volcanic rock treasure room, stores silk and damask vestments and 16th-century wooden sculptures.

Almost directly across the street is **Casa de Colón**, Colón 1, tel: 31-23-73 (weekdays 9am–6pm, weekends 9am–3pm). It's a beautiful, 12-room house set around twin courtyards with models of Las Palmas in different eras, nautical maps, navigational instruments, charts of Columbus' journeys, paintings on loan from Madrid's Prado museum... and two noisy parrots guarding an ancient well.

On the far corner of the square, you will find the CICA, the art gallery cum museum/conference centre run by the Caja de Ahor-

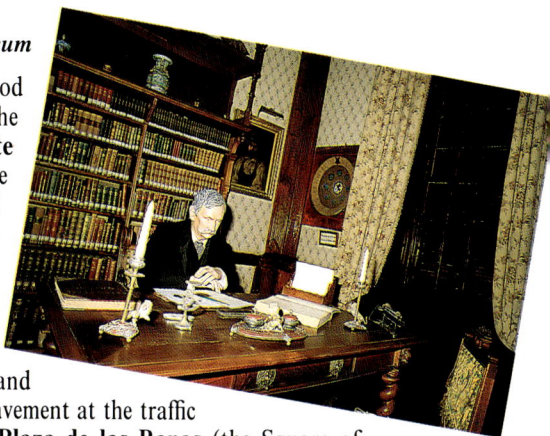

The Pérez Galdós Museum

ros (Savings Bank), a good venue for exhibitions. The **Centro Atlantico de Arte Moderno (CAAM)**, Calle de Los Balcones 9, tel: 31 18 24 (Tuesday to Saturday 10am–9pm, Sunday 10am–2pm) concentrates on the work of young Canarian artists.

Retrace your steps and cross over to the other pavement at the traffic lights for the so-called **Plaza de las Ranas** (the Square of the Frogs) with its checkerboard tiles and overhanging trees. Then make your way down Calle Peregrina and out onto Calle Malteses. Turn down to the right and take the first left for Calle Cano and the **Casa-Museo Pérez Galdós**, Cano 6, tel: 36 69 76 (weekdays 9am–1pm and 4–8pm). Among the many rooms is a reproduction of Benito Pérez Galdós' Santander study with furniture designed by the author and playwright himself. There are also hundreds of books, his own and those of Goethe, Dickens, Balzac, Tolstoy and Zola among others, many autographed by their authors. Galdós' skills as a historian and journalist have been compared to those of Charles Dickens of whom he was an admirer (he translated *The Pickwick Papers*). Among his own work, the novels *Fortunata* and *Jacinta* are published in English by Penguin Classics.

Stroll along Calle Cano until it meets Viera y Clavijo, observing the variety of architectural styles in this district including splendid examples of art nouveau and modernism. Look out for **Sayme**

Museums and Galleries

250 m / 272 yds

and **Madelca**, both of which sell modern prints by local artists. In Viera y Clavijo, there is a tempting cake shop and delicatessen **Morales**. Try a *sandwich de berros* (a watercress sandwich) or one of the many delicious sweets on display.

Three blocks ahead on Bravo Murillo is the classic modernist building of the **Cabildo,** and next door the **Centro Insular de Cultura** (weekdays 9am–2pm and 5–8pm), where you will sometimes find an exhibition showing traditional crafts, photography, art or architecture.

Back uptown (get off bus number 1 outside Hotel Santa Catalina) don't overlook the **Museo Néstor** in Parque Doramas – *see Itinerary 1, page 25*. On Calle Leon y Castillo, closer to Parque Santa Catalina, is the **La Regenta** gallery (Calle León y Castillo, 427; Monday to Friday 11am–1pm and 6–9pm) which stages a range of excellent exhibitions by Canary artists and photographers.

7. Shopping in Las Palmas

Breakfast on Parque Santa Catalina followed by best buys – from silk blouses to electric gadgets – in Las Canteras.

Las Palmas is a duty-free port, so you can find goods from all parts of the world here and at bargain prices. There are three main shopping areas.

The first area, where I suggest you spend the morning, lies in the part of Las Palmas behind Parque Santa Catalina (between the port and the beach): this is commonly referred to as **Las Canteras**. The second is **Triana** where the Canary islanders shop and where the most 'typical' souvenirs related to Canary culture can be bought (see *Itinerary 1*). The third is the area around **Mesa y López**, halfway between Triana and Las Canteras and dominated by the two big branches of the department store **El Corte Inglés**. This is the best place to shop for clothes.

Start off with a fortifying breakfast on one of the terraces on the **Parque Santa Catalina**. Ask for *chocolate con churros,* pastries that are dunked into thick hot chocolate – a typically Spanish start to the day. Beginning the day here has other advantages too, among

them the opportunity to pay an early call to the tourist office (which closes at 2pm). You're also conveniently close to both the port and the **Playa de las Canteras** which has a predictable array of souvenir shops selling postcards and other ephemera.

After breakfast, set off up **Calle Ripoche**, off the middle of the square. This is 'haggling' territory where you can pick up real bargains if you know how to strike a mean deal. Most of these shops are owned by Hindus who, although born and brought up in Las Palmas, have not lost their own culture's traditions and habits. One lingering superstition is that, if their first customer walks out of the shop empty-handed, things will not go well all day. Many of these immigrants bless their establishment by sprinkling the entrance with holy water from the Ganges – witness **Perry's** in the Calle Luis Morote.

On the third corner on the left in Ripoche is **Bazar Mavi,** excellent value for silk blouses and intricately crocheted tops. The tablecloths are also extremely good value. **Visanta**, a little further up on the left past the Levis shops, is one of the cheapest places for good quality cameras, watches, Ray-Ban sunglasses and electronic gear. Bargain hard.

Come out of Visanta and walk back down Ripoche in the direction of the Parque. This area of rundown shops and boarding houses is a favourite haunt of soldiers and sailors on leave from military service. There are some ethnic – particularly Indian – restaurants around here too, as well as numerous snack bars and a handful of inexpensive *pensiones*. It's not the best of areas to roam alone late at night, however. I cannot recommend that you check out specific shops here, as in an area such as this nothing is forever – what can be guaranteed is that as one store closes down, another one invariably leaps in to take its place – and the mix of electronics, jewellery, clothes and novelties remains roughly the same.

Gran Canaria is one of the best places to buy leatherwear and fur coats, all of excellent quality and at superb prices. There is little demand among islanders – though on opening nights of opera, you will see a great many furs around the Teatro Pérez Galdós – so most trade comes from holidaymakers. **Peletería Helena** (Luis Morote, parallel to Ripoche) offers high

Shoppers in Triana

quality clothes, with coats and jackets made to measure. A little further up Luis Morote, still on the left, **M Nanwani** specialises in arts and crafts from all parts of the world.

For great gifts, try **Marfil Dani** on the other side of Luis Morote, opposite **Zorba's** the disco. Lucky pyramids, children's watches, even football fans (of the ventilating type) are all found here. For more trinkets, drop in to **Napoleon**, beside the Hotel Concorde on Tomás Miller (the first street on your right off Luis Morote).

Although not typical of the Canary Islands, **Lladró** porcelain is much sought after and heavily taxed on the mainland. The shop which offers the best selection of Lladró is **Nara**, also good value for spirits and tobacco, on the corner of Tomás Miller and the beach. Opposite this shop, on the beachfront, is a useful beach shop, **Praia do Rio**, which has the best in Brazilian beachwear at cheap prices. Next door (Alfredo L Jones, 42) is **Fashion Beach**.

Further down Alfredo Jones (pronounced 'hoanies' by the locals), on the right hand side is **Electronica Bel**, purveyor of luxury sheets – even silk ones if you feel so inclined – Habana Club rum (not available everywhere) and good cigars. Still hankering after a tablecloth? Cross over to **Artesanía Paquita** where you can buy the real thing, which is Canary drawn-thread embroidery work, highly expensive, or alternativley a much cheaper Chinese replica. Again, try to bargain.

Lastly, hop in to either **Lurueña** or **Lopez** (one on each corner) for classic footwear and the latest fashions respectively.

If after all that shopping you only want a light lunch, try **La Cafetera** (back up Alfredo Jones, opposite the Reina Isabel Hotel); its crêpes and cakes are so delicious that you may end up eating more than you planned. Good value for money is **La Strada**, up Tomás Miller on the left-hand side (cross back over Luis Morote). It offers an excellent self-service buffet where you can eat as much as you like for relatively few pesetas.

Elegant shopping, traditional-style

The South

The south of Gran Canaria is known for its beaches, and tourist development is extensive. Nonetheless there are many villages and coves (for example Tasarte, Tasartico and Veneguera) untouched by tourism. As a rule, native Gran Canarians tend to prefer the beaches of San Agustín, Las Meloneras and Montaña Arena.

Sun, Sea and Sand

8. Playa del Inglés and Maspalomas

This itinerary introduces the main resort area of the south, taking in the lively shopping malls of Playa del Inglés and a walk along the ridge of the Dunes of Maspalomas. Relax over a buffet lunch/dinner at the Oasis or Rey Carlos hotels, or stay overnight in the hills at Tablero.

–From Las Palmas buses 05 and 50 go to Maspalomas faro (lighthouse) via Playa del Inglés (San Fernando stop); bus number 30 goes to Maspalomas via Playa del Inglés (Yumbo stop); bus 31 goes to Puerto Rico via Playa del Inglés (San Fernando); and bus 61 goes to Puerto Mogan via Playa del Inglés (San Fernando) and Puerto Rico.–

The South of Gran Canaria is a world apart. It caters for tourists who come in search of sun, sea, sand and organised entertainment, which is here aplenty. Remains of Guanches were found here during excavations for the motorway, but they have been whisked out of public sight until the powers-that-be decide their fate. Itinerary 9, which can be followed from the main resort area, will take you away from the crowds to look at the Guanche and Roman heritage as well as beautiful countryside. Itinerary 8 highlights the best of Playa del Inglés and Maspalomas, whilst itineraries 10 and 11 sample the South's varied entertainments and leisure activities.

From the highway, the big (and often unaesthetic) hotels along the south coast appear to be merely a concrete jungle, but on closer inspection **Playa del Inglés** and **Maspalomas** – which run into each other – give the impression of a vast suburb. Skirting the highway at the northern end is the district of **San Fernando**, its commercial centre (one vast shopping mall) at the southeast corner. Across the traffic circle, Cruz de San Fernando, is the post office from which the mile-long **Avenida de Tirajana** leads down to the beach with a supermarket on what seems to be every corner between endless hotels, restaurants and tacky shops.

There are numerous other malls, notably **Yumbo** (turn left at the

C.d.Tirma

Mirador
de Balcón Andén Verde Montaña
Altavista
1376 Moriscos
1771

Puerto de
la Aldea Cruz de Tejeda
1450

Punta de
la Aldea Tejeda

Presa del
El Parailllo

Presa
del Caidero
de las Niñas Roque
Bentaiga

San Nicolás
de Tolentino Los Molinos El Toscon Roque
Nublo
1700

Presa de
Siberio El Fraile

El Montañe

PLAYA
DE
GÜIGÜI Inagua
1426 Cuevas
de Pajonales

Cueva de
las Niñas

Tasarte

Presa de
Soria Embalse
de Chira San B
de

Las Casas
de Veneguera

PLAYA
DE
ASNO Pie de
Cuesta

Santa Brígida

Barranco de Tasarte Casas
El Inglés Mogán

Punta
Rabelago Barranco Veneguera Embalse
de Ayaguares

La Playa
de Veneguera Tabaibales

Los Palmitos
Park

B. de Arguineguin

La Playa de Mogán Taurito

Presa de
Chamoriscan

Puerto de
Mogán Tauro

LA PLAYA DE TAURO

Puerto Rico

Patalavaca Cornisa Las
Casas Las Meloneras

Montaña
Arena

Arguineguin Pasito
Blanco Oasis de
Maspalomas

Atlantic Ocean Bahía de
S.Agueda

PLAYA LAS
MELONERAS

The South
4 km / 2.5 miles

Plaza Arucas) in which the tourist office is situated, and **Cita** (turn left at Plaza Agaete). Wandering around these two-level malls is the major occupation in these parts and can be quite entertaining. In Yumbo especially, in addition to banks, game arcades and scores of shops including a Macy's selling only sports clothes, there must be at least 50 restaurants. Each shares a wall with the next and

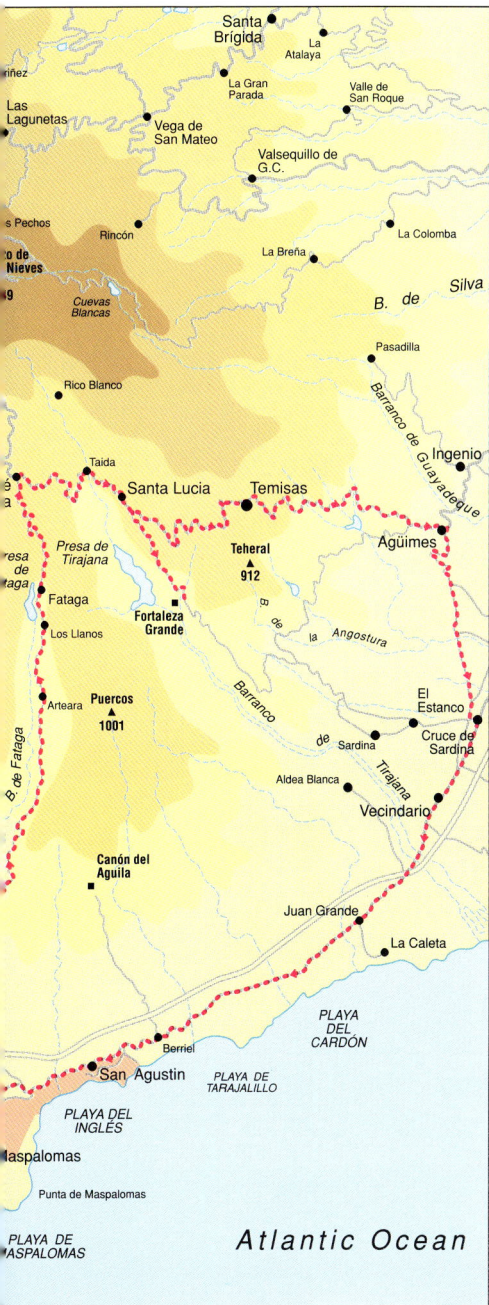

differentiates itself by exhibiting coloured drinks, fish on ice, slabs of meat or life-size cardboard cut-out figures. All display menus in four languages. The malls are just as busy at night because numerous nightclubs and bars are also situated therein.

Just above Plaza Agaete is the campy **Hotel Rey Carlos**, its tropical garden guarded by nude statues and plastic-armoured Don Quixote clones. It's worth seeing and you can relax in the hotel's comfortable lounge or partake of its very reasonable all-you-can-eat dinners (6–9pm, tables fill by 6.15pm).

The bottom of Tirajana is blocked off by the massive RIU **Palace**, a luxury hotel whose poolside gardens are filled with affluent, overweight, predominantly German couples many of whom rarely leave the enclosed premises. A block to the east is access to the beach from the which the hotel appears as a sprawling Moorish palace on the skyline.

Southern bathing belle

The beach is actually the **Dunes of Maspalomas**, one of the oddest sights on the island, and the subject of innumerable photographs. The dunes reach heights of about 10m (30–40ft) above the 'valleys' below them , and stretch for about a mile westwards to the Maspalomas lighthouse. They are best negotiated by following a circuitous route atop the ridges rather than climbing up and down. It is shorter and easier, of course, to head down to the sea and walk along the beach.

From the Hotel Palm Beach, walk north beside the Barranco de Maspalomas to where it meets the main road beside City Hall and the police headquarters. Just beyond, there's a stop for buses back to Playa del Inglés and the quieter resort of **San Augustin** which adjoins it on the east side. Most of the buses that extensively network this trio of resorts head onwards to Las Palmas. Bus number 60 stops on the highway outside the airport.

While still in Maspalomas, you may wish to make use of the **Maspalomas Golf Course** (18 holes), Avenida Africa (tel: 76 25 81). Golf clubs can be hired if you don't have your own. Å good place for lunch, after you have worked up an appetite playing golf or walking along the dunes, is in the unforgettable surroundings of the **Oasis Hotel** restaurant (near the lighthouse). The daily buffet lunch is reasonably priced and the gardens, with their strutting peacocks and waving palm trees, are beautifully landscaped – perfect, in fact, for an after-lunch snooze.

The vast majority of tourists who arrive in the Maspalomas/Playa del Inglés area are already booked into accommodation on cheap package tours and the hotels they use are rarely a bargain for the individual traveller. Except for the Christmas period, the aforementioned Hotel Carlos Rey is a good choice, and a list of other hotels, pensions and bungalows

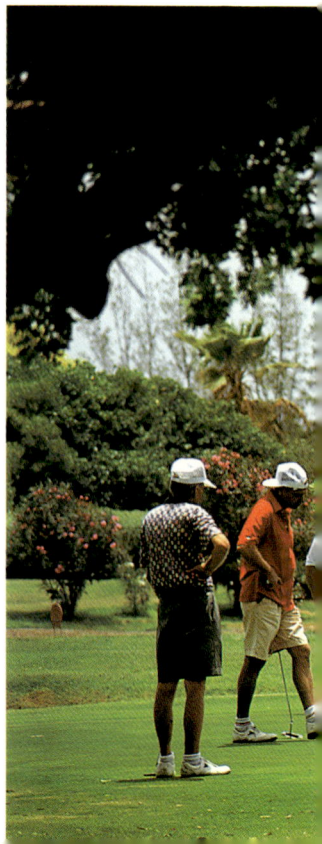

for rent is available from the tourist office in Playa del Inglés: Centro Insular de Turismo, Yumbo Centre, Avenida Espana y Ave EEU, tel: 928-76 25 91, fax: 76 78 48.

An interesting alternative is to stay up in the hills, a mile above Maspalomas, in the village of **Tablero** where the **Pension Alvarez** (Sergio, the owner, speaks English) has simple, clean rooms for about £10 per person. There are several bars and cafes, an inexpensive Chinese restaurant and the superb gourmet restaurant, **A. Gaudi**.

Waiting for a bite

If you wander into the modern municipal auditorium at the lower end of town, especially at weekends, you might be able to catch a five-a-side football match taking place. A new industrial estate is arising in the west, but from the east side of town you can look down into the canyon that leads to **Palmitos Park** and see Aqua Sur (a water park playground) and the Go Kart track. Unfortunately, the cliff is far too steep to get down.

The 44 bus between Las Palmas and Maspalomas calls at Tablero hourly between 7am and 7pm; otherwise the taxi ride is inexpensive.

On the lonely strand at Güigüi

9. Exploring the South

As a change from your resort, I recommend a drive or bus trip from Playa del Inglés into an area of dramatic scenery, with visits to an historical tableau and Roman museum, and the opportunity to eat at a cave restaurant and go camel riding. Having completed a round trip, you can continue westwards along the coast, through Playa del Inglés and on to Puerto Rico and Mogán.

–From Playa del Inglés (San Fernando) bus number 18 to San Bartolomé goes through Arteara and Fataga and continues onward to Cruz de Tejeda. See map on page 50–

About 16km (10 miles) north of Playa del Inglés, in the Barranco de Fataga, is **Mundo Aborigen**, which through 100 lifesize figures in a variety of settings tries to tell the unhappy story of the original Canarian natives, the Guanches – who in the 15th century fought the Spanish invaders almost to the last man and were finally finished off by a plague (see *Itinerary 10*)

In 1590, the Italian architect Leonardo Torriani reported that these early Canarians 'lived without knowing or feeling illness, at least until they reached the age of 120 or 140 .Although their health may also in part be ascribed to the perfection and mildness of the air, yet the main reason must lie in the modest range of foodstuffs, none discordant with another, on which they lived – only barley, boiled, steamed or roast meat, milk and butter, all of which contribute to human health.'

At **Arteara** is the **Mesón de la Silla**, a cave restaurant that opens onto a terrace offering inspiring views over what looks like a condensed version of the Grand Canyon; this is the sort of scenery that the Canarian poet Miguel de Unamuno described as 'petrified storm'. (see *Itinerary 4*).

In a palm-filled oasis between Arteara and the sweet little village of **Fataga** you can go camel riding on a short safari that ends with food and drinks. About 8km (5 miles) further north, in the centre of a fruit growing (and brandy-making) area, is San Bartolomé de Tirajana, from which the bus heads onwards to the *posada* at Cruz de Tejeda.

If you don't want to go back the same way, bus number 34 (infrequent) heads east through **Santa Lucía**, an attractive town with an interesting mu-

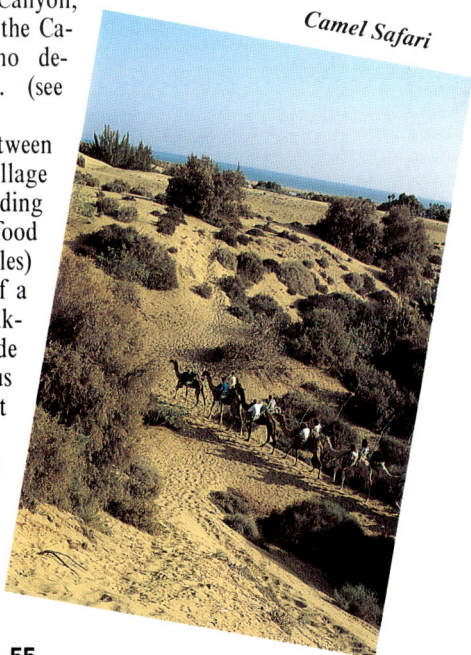

Camel Safari

Into the canyons

Canary wrestling

seum, and onwards to Agüimes. One of the museum's attractions is a 3rd-century Roman amphora which was recovered from the sea off the neighbouring island of Lanzarote.

The Canary Islands were well known to the Romans who were securely established on the nearby Moroccan coast. Pliny (62–113 AD) referred to them as 'Canaria, so called from the multitude of dogs of great size', and long before this Homer's reference to the Elysian Fields (*There is no snow, no winter storm, no pouring rain/And there is ever heard the murmur of the softly-breathing West/Which Ocean sends to bring men gentle coolness*) is usually thought to refer to the Canary Islands. And the 2nd-century writer Plutarch called them 'the Isles of the Blessed. Seldom watered by moderate showers of rain, most commonly by gentle dew-bringing winds...'

South of Santa Lucía, the castle-shaped rock **Fortaleza Grande**, was a sacred spot to the Guanches – their final refuge during the Spanish conquest of the late 15th century.

Heading west along the south coast is an interesting trip. Bus number 39 from Playa del Inglés (Yumbo) goes to Puerto Rico in the morning and buses 38 (infrequent) from Las Palmas to San Nicolas and 01 from Las Palmas to Puerto de Mogán both stop at Playa del Inglés. **Puerto Rico**, situated where a canyon meets the sea, is famous for fishing and sailing but doesn't have much else to offer. Except, that is, for the ride to Puerto de Mogán in Manuel Baer's glass-bottomed *Blue Bird*, which you'll find moored beside the pleasant café Las Caracolas. Lineas Salmon also operates boat along the coast. At 10.30am daily the Windjammer San Miguel leaves the port for an all-day cruise.

Gone fishing

At **Puerto de Mogán** the buildings are mercifully low-rise and – judging by the ubiquitous chalkboard menus – most of the tourists are German. Development has only been partial, for there's just one hotel, though lots of apartments: the 56-room **Club de Mar**, which has a restaurant and a poolside bar.

Evening at Puerto de Mogán

To continue around the island it's necessary to head inland past the avocado plantations to the village of **Mogán** itself (bus number 84 runs over the route four times daily), and although side trips can be made back down roads to the coast, notably to **Veneguera**, the roads are not always good, especially to the less-visited beaches of **Tasarte** and **Tasartico**. Of course, for some people, fnding a deserted beach is worth any trouble. The fact is that this whole region has been the subject of sometimes bitter battles for years, with environmentalists fighting to preserve its pristine solitude and developers seeking to make money.

Mogán has become a popular hideout for artists and writers. There are rooms for rent – ask for suggestions at the Eucalyptus bar opposite the minimart – and there are two highway restaurants. These are situated on the way to San Nicolás and below the magnificent mountains fringed with trees – a curious section of hillside striated with brilliant shades of orange, green and brown.

The **Mirador el Balcon**, an observation point on the highway, offers spectacular views (and the ubiquitous snack-serving truck) as does the **Anden Verde** ('green platform') further along the coast from which Agaete can be seen. Visitors invariably rave about the stupendous views from this section of the northwest coast.

San Nicolás de Tolentino is famous for its tomatoes, grown with the aid of numerous mountain reservoirs, but has begun to suffer from the competition from Moroccan growers so that the dumping of surplus crops has become all too common. The population is consequently dropping.

The highway heads down the *barranco* to the coast, where it continues on to Agaete. From San Nicolas, Utinsa bus 101 runs back to Las Palmas via Gáldar three times a day.

This is not so much an itinerary as a round-up of attractions you may want to try when the beach becomes a bore and you've had enough of exploring. It includes a bird park with parrot shows, two water parks, a Western theme park and places to try go-karting or play golf.

—To reach the Go Kart park, Aqua Sur, and Palmitas park beyond, take the number 45 bus from Playa del Inglés (Yumbo); bus 29 from Yumbo goes to Sioux City —

There is a series of family attractions just a few miles out of Playa del Inglés. These include the **Go Kart** park and **Aqua Sur**, open every day from 10.30am, which has a number of huge pools with water-slides plus other attractions as well as restaurants and a souvenir shop. **Palmitos Park** is the island's major tourist attraction and with good reason. It has scores of beautiful birds, including many varieties of lorikeets and similar breeds from Australia and New Guinea, and many birds bred right here, as well as toucans, peacocks and flamingos. There are also monkeys, an aquarium, a butterfly enclosure, a cactus garden and a greenhouse filled with exotic orchids.

The path through the Palmitos Park winds gradually up the hillside, but the most popular exhibit is next to the cafeteria near the entrance. Here a team of well-trained parrots do a series of amusing (and amazing) tricks, from pushing a scooter across the stage with one leg to ringing a bell the number of times requested by a member of the audience. In addition, one or another of our feathered friends walks backwards, wags his tail, raises the EU flag, fits oddly shaped jigsaw pieces into place, drives a mini bus, slides down a ramp, rollerskates, rolls over dead after playing the part of *toro* in a bullfight, pedddles a bicycle across a high wire and lies back in a deckchair wearing sunglasses and holding a paper. Among the items sold in the park's souvenir shop are tiny carved parrots on sticks and a booklet describing the hundreds of plant species from all parts of the world.

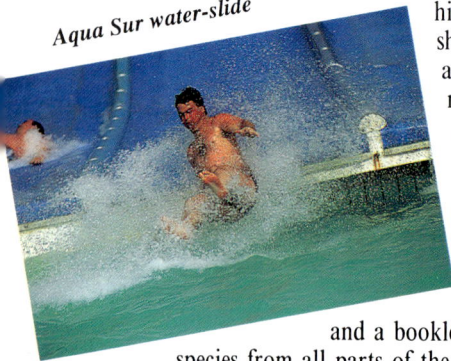

Aqua Sur water-slide

Taking a different route inland from Playa del Inglés on bus 29, through Aguila canyon, you can visit **Sioux City**. This is a fabulous reproduction of an old cowboy town with sagging wooden buildings and sandy streets. Half a dozen buffalo idle languidly on the site of a projected Indian village and a looped tape heavy on Dolly Parton and Roger Miller plays nonstop. Twice a day visitors abandon the stores selling Western clothes or having their pictures taken for 'Wanted' posters and file into the saloon to consume beer and sandwiches while they watch a show which consists mainly of rope spinning and hair-raising knife throwing at a human target.

Afterwards, visitors can take horseback rides up and down Main Street where another show is staged: based around a bank hold-up, dramatic falls from rooftops, the capture and stringing up of the outlaw, etc. With exquisite timing the (passengerless) bus leaves for Maspolomas when this is still going on. The next bus is one hour later. On Friday nights, Sioux City stages a big show in its 1,000-seat stadium, followed by a barbecue.

In Maspolomas itself the major attraction is **Ocean Park**, serviced by most of the buses on Avenida Tirajana, and including another water park, an amusement park called Holiday World (opens 6pm) with sealion and parrot shows, and the adjoining Maspolomas Golf Course where clubs and equipment can be hired.

Further afield are the **Gran Karting Club** at Tarajalillo, east of San Augustin; **Cocodrilos Park**, near Agüimes, which also features exotic animals (hourly bus 9am–2pm from outside Hotel Rey Carlos); and **Mundo Aborigen**, a theme park dedicated to explaining the life of the Guanches, the earliest inhabitants of the Canary Islands who were pretty much extinct by early in the 16th century. The park sheds light on their fascinating Stone Age society in which women fought alongside men in battle and had an equal role in running Guanche affairs, and adulterers were said to have been buried alive. A visit to Mundo Aborigen can be incorporated into Itinerary 9.

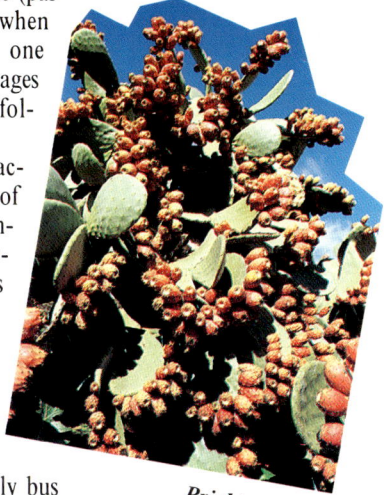

Prickly flowers

The Maspalomas sand dunes

11. Water Sports and Fishing Trips

Charter a boat or hire a guide to take you deep-sea fishing or fish for a shark; take a ferry or excursion boat to sightsee from the water. An assortment of water sports is also on offer: waterskiing, windsurfing, diving and others.

You will need to organise your day on the water with care; you are restricted by Spanish sailing laws that oblige you to hire someone to pilot your boat as well as hiring the boat itself. Check exactly what you will get – although there are lots of people offering this service, they don't always give value for money. Make sure the person who takes you out is insured.

Conditions in Gran Canaria are excellent for year-round deep-sea game fishing, with tuna, bonito and swordfish usually prevalent. The marinas at **Pasito Blanco**, **Puerto Rico** and **Mogán** all offer sports fishing opportunities from such boats as *Dorado* (tel: 56 55 21), *Blue Marlin* (tel: 56 50 71), *Barakuda* (tel: 73 50 80) and *Carmen* (tel: 75 30 13).

If you prefer something more adventurous, try shark fishing. The best place for chartering your own boat (six people minimum/eight maximum) is Puerto Rico, round the far side of the marina. Telephone bookings are not accepted, but they say Tuesday and Friday are less busy. You can choose between two timetables: 9am–3.30pm or 3.30–8pm. If you want to fish it costs from 6,000ptas; if you only want to watch, it costs a bit less.

If you don't mind an organised trip in the company of rather more people, you can get a cheaper deal. The *Punta Umbría II* (tel: 26 82 80) at the entrance to the marina offers breakfast, lunch, shark fishing, coffee and brandy, with a stop at a small cove along the way (children under 10 half-price), Monday to Wednesday and weekends 11am–4.30pm). The return coach transfer from your resort is included in the price.

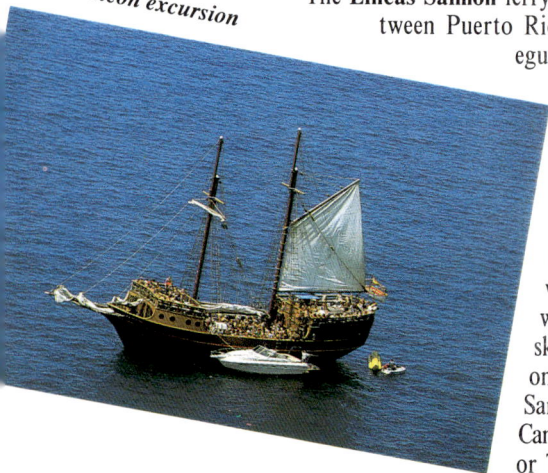

Galleon excursion

The **Líneas Salmon** ferry (tel: 24 37 08) runs between Puerto Rico, Mogán and Arguineguin about every half hour.

Trips on the *Golden Submarine* start from behind the **Club del Mar** complex (tel: 56 56 56) in Mogán.

Those who prefer to keep their head above water can learn to sail, windsurf, dive or waterski, as well as taking a trip on an excursion boat – try San Miguel (tel: 76 00 76), Canarias Charter (tel: 569 44) or Tamarix (tel: 603 216).

Shopping

There are lots of things to buy as souvenirs of Gran Canaria. Where you buy depends upon what you are after. Shops open at 10am, close between 2–4pm or 4.30pm, and close again around 8pm. Large stores such as **El Corte Inglés**, **Galerías Preciados** and **Zara**, all in the Mesa y López area, never close at lunchtime and others, such as **Maya** (Triana; tel: 37 20 49), stay open all day during festivals, for example between Christmas and 6 January.

The largest shopping centre in Las Palmas is on Calle Paria in the north of the city: **Las Arenas** (tel: 27 70 08), with boutiques, restaurants and cinemas. In total, there are more than 100 shops which open until 10pm (until 2pm Sunday).

Many of the handicrafts produced in the Canary Islands are unique to this region of Spain – such items as banana leaf baskets, woven silk and *chácaras* (large chunky castanets). Embroidered tablecloths are produced in many places, including **Teror**, which is also renowned for its baskets. **Arucas**, **Atalaya** and **Santa Brígida** are especially known for their pottery and **Guia** for its bone-handled knives.

In Las Palmas, items which are representative of Canary culture are found mainly between **Calle Armas** in Vegueta or in the **Fataga** shops, one of which is in the Pueblo Canario (see *Itinerary 1*) and the other in the Parque Santa Catalina. The Calle Armas establishment is especially good for *naifes* (knifes with goathorn handles, originally used by workers in the banana fields), which start off at around 6,000ptas. You can also buy *naife* brooches or even earrings. In wood, you can buy miniature replicas of *balcones canarios* (the famous wooden balconies), *arcones* (caskets), elaborately chiselled picture frames and *pilas*, tiny replicas of the

filter stone traditionally used to collect water. The musical instruments on offer are *chacaras* (very big castanets), *timples* (very small guitars) and an odd collection of bones hung on goatskin (which works

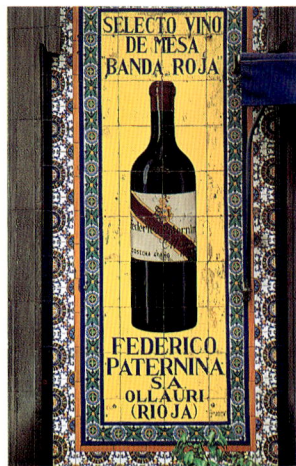

Not for taking home!

in a similar way to a washboard). In basketry, there are elaborate cane birdcages and typical local hats and baskets of all shapes and sizes. Earthenware includes the famous *ídolos de Tara*, *cachimbas* (clay pipes) and *pintaderas* (clay seals fashioned into brooches).

In the Fataga shops you will also find lace handkerchiefs, placemats and little figures dressed in the various native costumes of the different islands. Shop assistants will pack items so that they can be easily transported in suitcases.

Fedac (full name: Fundación para la Etnografía y Desarollo de la Artesania Canaria) is a government-sponsored store at Calle Domingo J. Navarro 7 (tel: 38 23 60), off the Avenida de Triana. It has by far the best selection of native handicrafts (see *Itinerary 1*).

Atarecos, Calle Peregrina 4, tel: 38 23 60, is a small shop tightly packed with Canarian handicrafts and all manner of other fascinating items.

If you want to buy Canary music, visit the music department in the Corte Inglés (Mesa y López). If it is classical music that you want, buy the *Cantos Canarios* by Teobaldo Power or anything by the modern composer Falcón Sanabria. For folk music, the best representatives are **Los Sabandeños**, **Mestisay** or **Los Gofiones**. In more modern music, the **Parranda Cuasquías** and **Los Coquillos** are among the best.

The Mesa y López area is particularly good for clothes, with shops such as **Cortefiel**, **D'roma**, **Mango**, **Prenatal** (for children's clothes) and **Zara** offering a wide range of possibilities to suit all pockets. Shoe shops abound. You will find **Lurueña** and **López** again but also **Don Juan** at the bottom end of the street.

For anything in the way of cameras, computer games, etc, try **Maya** in Triana, which, unlike the other Indian shops where the custom is to haggle, offers reasonable prices with a guarantee. For souvenirs, look out for the gold *pintaderas* or the little gold replicas of Gran Canaria.

Canary lace

Local flowers

Canary tobacco is another popular purchase. Apart from the cigars, either in stacks from **La Palma** or in boxes (**Condal**), both of which can be purchased in the Canteras shops or in the Corte Inglés, the most popular strong tobacco is **Coronas,** but the strongest of the strong is **Kruger** or **Mecánicos**, both of which come without filters and are rough. More specialty cigar stores can be found on Calles Quintana, Ripoche and Albareda.

For wine, try the malmseys from Lanzarote. **El Grifo is** the best white wine and **Malvasía** the best rosé. As a rule, red wines are not recommended: *Vino del Monte*, which you can buy in local bars in the Tafira and La Atalaya areas, is an acquired taste.

Weekends are market days in Teror, Santa Brígida and San Mateo, when stalls are filled with handicrafts as well as bread and cakes, dried fish, honey and loal cheeses. In Las Palmas, a wide range of cheeses can be found at **CVumbres Canarias**, Avenida de las Escaleritas 43, tel: 20 45 36.

The lively **Mercado de Vegueta**, at the lowest part of the old town, specialises in fish, meat, fruit and vegetables and is surrounded by more stalls and lots of street activity. At the other end of town (where the northbound number 1 bus makes its final turn) is the **Mercado del Puerto** on Calle Alberede. It closes at 2pm.

For tourists with a sweet tooth, boxes of *turron duro de almendra* (delicious almond nougat) can be found in any supermarket, and all over Las Palmas are shops specialising in hundreds of types of candy, chocolate and nuts (for example, **Casa Ricardo** — see *Itinerary 1*).

Eating Out

Very little remains of the of the ancient cuisine of the earliest Canarians – their staple dish being the rather insipid *gofio* (toasted ground corn) – so traditional fare is predominantly what arrived with the Spaniards. Nevertheless, the Canary Islands have a cuisine all of their own, making extensive use of vegetables which are produced here in abundance.

Island cheeses are often made from goat's milk and are dictinctive. Guia's *queso de flor* (with a mild flavour) is much prized, but if you like strong cheese try the *majorero* made from cow's milk (from Fuerteventura). Olive trees proliferate so, as in mainland Spain, olive oil is a familiar ingredient and olives are combined with the local *sauce mojo* and served with various dishes. Herbs and spices are widely used, especially garlic, paprika, marjoram, thyme, saffron, cumin, cloves and fresh coriander.

Special today

As for fresh, locally produced meats, there is goat and rabbit – try the succulent *conejo al salmorejo* (rabbit in hot chilli sauce). *Baifo* is the term for succulent young kid. Other specialities of the region include *potaje de berros* (water-cress soup) with *gofio* (toasted cornflour) and *caldo de pescado* (fish and vegetables with a coriander sauce and *gofio*).

Fish understandably plays a large part in the Canarian diet, with 'mero vieja', 'abae' and 'cherne' (a kind of bass) especially popular. Salt cherne is the main ingredient in the traditional dish of *sancocho* (fish boiled with potatoes and served with *gofio*). Vieja (not unlike parrotfish) is usually poached and served with *mojo* (a garlicky sauce) and coriander. As its name implies, it is an ancient fish, said to have originated in the Aegean many millennia ago. Sama, a type of seabream, is also served with *mojo verde*, and is especially recommended. A delicious accompaniment to fish or cheese is *papas arrugadas* (small salty jacket potatoes) served with *mojo picón* (hot chilli sauce).

Vegetarians are well catered for. *Ropa vieja* (literally 'old clothes') is chick-peas with diced potatoes and other vegetables (though be careful, meat is sometimes slipped in too). *Moros y cristianos* (literally, Moors and Christians) is white rice with kidney beans. Salads make full use of fruits: for example, *aguacate* (avocado) and melon are mixed together with papaw and strawberries.

There was once a flourishing wine industry on Gran Canaria, but this has withered away over the years and now vines are cultivated only in a small area in El Monte. At Arucas, 50,000 litres of Arehucas rum are distilled daily from local sugar cane.

With regard to Canarian desserts, if you have a sweet tooth, try the *bienmesabe* (a honey and almond confection) and the *turrón* (a kind of nougat).

Eating out is cheap. As with most things, the south is more expensive, in spite of the competition. In the list that follows, $ indicates a meal costing less than 2,500ptas for one person (drinks extra); $$ under 8,000ptas; and $$$ up to 15,000ptas.

Should you feel dubious about trying local food or just feel in need of a change occasionally, Chinese restaurants abound. One or two Indian restaurants have also opened up — **Nan Kima** and **Restaurant Polar**, Calle Sagasta 17, have cheap Indian food including vegetarian — and there are three Japanese establishments. The newest Japanese is beside the bus station at San Telmo and is excellent value for money. A Russian restaurant, **La Balailaika** (Guanarleme) also offers wonderful food at great prices.

Basic ingredients

Las Palmas and the North

Canary Cuisine

CA'CHO DAMIAN
León y Castillo, 26, Las Palmas
Tel: 365323
Choose from a tempting array of enormous bowls on the counter or opt for the set menu. Visa accepted. $$

EL HERREÑO
Mendizabal, 5–7, Las Palmas
Tel: 310513
The set menu is usually tempting but if not try a mixture of dishes in *raciones*. Try the *churros de pescado* (fish in batter) and the *carajaca* (liver). Ask for wine from El Hierro: the rosé is the best (*rosado*). No credit cards. $

PEPE EL BRECA
Gumindafe 32, Las Palmas
Tel: 468065
This is the fish restaurant *par excellence*. The best in Canary cuisine. Allow the owners to advise you on what to choose. Book in advance or be prepared to wait

with a drink. All credit cards accepted. $$$

LAS GRUTAS DE ARTILES
Las Meleguinas s/n, Santa Brígida (Centre)
Tel: 640575/641250
Built into caves 11km (7 miles) outside Las Palmas, the food is typically Canary. Recommended for a romantic night out, but avoid Saturdays, when wedding and first communion parties are invariably installed. Visa, Mastercard accepted. $$

Spanish Food (Regional)

AMAIUR
Pérez Galdós, 2, Las Palmas
Tel: 370717
Imaginative dishes from the Basque country, one of the greatest gastronomic regions of Spain. Expect to rub shoulders with local politicians since the restaurant lies across the road from the Government offices in San Bernardo. All credit cards accepted. $$$

EL PADRINO
J.Nazareno, 1, Las Coloradas,

Fresh fish

Las Palmas
Tel: 272094
Seafood. Fresh fish served in pleasant out-of-town surroundings with fine views over Las Canteras. Especially recommended is *parrillada de pescado*, an enormous dish of grilled fish, washed down with the white wine El Grifo from Lanzarote. All credit cards accepted. $$

DON QUIJOTE
S Artiles 74, Las Palmas
Tel: 272786
Great fondues, crêpes and *carne a la piedra* – stone-grilled meats you cook yourself. The wine on the table – as opposed to the table wine – can usually be recommended. Visa accepted. $$

CANGURO
C Travieso 27, Las Palmas
Tel: 366002
and C Venegas 23, Las Palmas
Tel: 366740
Both restaurants – in the same area – are recognisable by a wooden kangaroo at the door. The one in C Travieso (off Triana) is the quieter of the two. Food is well-priced and inventive. In particular, look out for the excellent fish which goes under the unpromising name of *burro* (donkey). Visa accepted. $$

EL SECUESTRO
Teror (centre)
Grilled meat, succulent *chorizo* and black puddings (*morcillas*) from Teror. Not for small appetites. The atmosphere is rustic. Always crowded on Sunday and holidays. Closed Monday. No credit cards. $

Other Cuisines

LA PASTA REAL
Secretario Padilla, 28,
Las Palmas
Tel: 262267
Italian and macrobiotic. The owner used to work in the Scottish town of St Andrew's and therefore speaks fluent English with a broad Scots accent. Service is excellent. The menu, chalked up on a blackboard, includes many delicious dishes. Visa, Diners accepted. $

LE FRANÇAIS
Sargento Llagas, 18, Las Palmas
Tel: 266762
Wonderful food from the great gastronomic regions of France. The desserts are mouthwatering. Visa, American Express accepted. $$

Cave restaurant, Barranco de Guayadequ

LAS TREBEDAS
6th floor, El Corte Inglés, Las Palmas
Tel: 272600
Menu in English. Wide selection includes fixed price lunch. $

HAMBURGO
Mary Sanchez 54, Las Palmas
Tel: 469745
Nice atmosphere wuth candles on tables and bric-a-brac covered walls (including a photo of owner Manuel alongside Spanish king Juan Carlos). Enormous German-style platters. $$

SOL BARDINOS CAFÉ
24th floor, Hotel Sol Bardinos, Eduardo Benot 3, Las Palmas
Hamburgers, sandwiches, chicken, fish, various entrées, all under 1000ptas. $

LA STRADA
Tomas Miller 58, Las Palmas
Tel: 273351
Buffet noon–11pm, 1350ptas. $

Among the selection of fast food establishments in Las Palmas is a chain called **TelePizza**, which delivers (tel: 221819). The main outlet is at Paseo de la Canteras and Calle Estevanez.

The South

Self-service restaurants with an all-you-can eat policy at a fixed price are prevalant in Playa del Inglés, with **Las Camelias**, Avenida de Tirajana 15, tel: 760236, and **Lapu Lapu**, Avenida Alferes Provisionales 33, being amog the most popular. The **Westfalia**, a terrace café in the Cita shopping centre, doesn't open until 9pm but always has music. **Bali**, Avenida Tirajana 23, specialises in Indonesian cuisine, while **Anno Domini** at the shopping centre in San Augustin has a reliable French menu.

PEPE EL BRECA II
Carretera de Fataga, Maspalomas
Tel: 772637
If you didn't make it to the original Pepe el Breca in Las Palmas (see *page 65*),

Buffet spread

don't miss this off-shoot, run by Pepe's daughter. The bass baked in salt is excellent. Typical Canary desserts. Slightly off the beaten track All credit cards accepted. $$

LA FAROLA
C Alcalá Galiano 3, Puerto de Arinaga
Tel: 180410
Upmarket establishment in the tiny port of Arinaga. Specialises in seafood. Relaxed ambience. All credit cards accepted. $$$

RIAS BAJAS
Edificio Playa Sol, Av de Tirajana, Playa del Inglés
Tel: 764033
This restaurant specialises in Galician cuisine, so seafood is a must. In particular, try the *empanada* (a kind of vegetable and tuna pie) and the *tarta de Santiago* (almond cake). Be guided by the chef. Visa, American Express accepted. $$

Seafood paella

Nightlife

Possibly one of the reasons for the Canary Islander's famous *aplatanamiento* (literally the 'state of becoming a banana') is that they love to stay out until all hours, dancing and making merry. If you decide to drop in on any of the special events, you will see how people go all out to have a good time even in the smallest village. Of course, the bigger the festivity, the more elaborate the celebration, but you can always count on finding *papagüevos* (giants on stilts or enormous-headed dwarves), a firework display and a *verbena*, a shindig in the village square with rollicking live music supplied by the local band. (Look out for the old faithfuls of the popular Banda de Agaete, an essential ingredient in any good celebration on Gran Canaria.)

The best thing about these celebrations is their community spirit. Apart from during the very few slow dances, everyone dances with everyone else, regardless of age or any other differences.

People usually drink beer or *cubalibre* at these events and no celebration is complete without the *tollos* and *pejines* (two kinds of salty fish with a texture like chewing-gum, guaranteed to give you a healthy thirst). This and Carnival are the only occasions when you are expected to pay as you drink. Note: it is advisable to keep your money in a waist pouch wise since handbags are cumbersome and wallets easily stolen.

If you are looking for something more sophisticated in the way of nightlife, then Gran Canaria is the place for you also. But be warned on two counts: nobody who has any pretensions to being cool goes out before midnight, and discos exist primarily for facilitating brief encounters with the opposite sex (in some cases women are admitted free to encourage their custom). The locals are not backward at coming forward and are always keen to practise their language skills – especially since the level of decibels in discos usually makes close proximity essential.

The music to dance to at the moment is *bakalao* and the in crowd do a circuit known as *la ruta del bakalao* (literally the 'cod route'), which winds up in **La Roca** in San Agustín, in the south of the island (the less energetic can drop into **La Quinta Avenida**, next door to La Roca). As with shops (see *Shopping, pages 62–3*), different areas offer different varieties of nightlife.

Las Palmas

In Las Palmas, in the area towards Vegueta and behind Triana (around Teatro Pérez Galdós), the bars are more restrained in style, designed for an 'older' young generation. This is totally in keeping with the general atmosphere of the

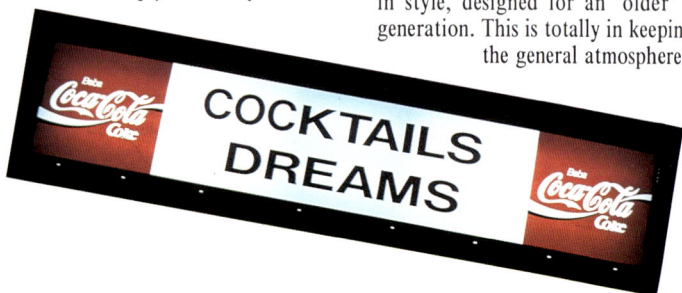

area, which is more relaxed and refined. Begin your evening here at around 11pm (take a taxi to the theatre), perhaps kicking off with **Gasquías** in the Calle San Pedro, behind the theatre, which offers live music, a pool table (as the name indicates) and pleasant company. **Yurfa** is another old favourite. Housed in an old Canary building in Calle Perdomo, this bar provides good music, art exhibitions, excellent prices and lots of quiet corners where you can sit down and talk without straining the vocal chords.

After midnight, the place to head is the **Plaza de la Victoria**, with its many noisy, bustling bars. Again, take a taxi. The neighbours who live above the pubs don't take kindly to spirited revellers so you are advised to stand under the protection of the awnings: more than one irate local has been known to 'water' the clientele gathered below.

Heineken is the golden-oldie of these tiny bars. The jukebox music is also mainly golden oldies. However, the latest place to be is **El Cinco**, another terraced bar in Plaza de la Victoria. If your idea of an enjoyable night on the town includes male strippers or wet T-shirts on Schwarzenegger lookalikes you may want to try **La Geiser** next door. **La Floridita** (near the Plaza de las Ranas; tel: 43 17 40) is tops. Reproducing a Havana nightclub, it doesn't wake up until very late.

Around 2am, you should be thinking of making a move towards El Puerto. If you are looking for glitz and glitter, then **Pachá**, behind the Saba car park and down on the harbour front, is the place to go. If you are feeling energetic, squeeze onto its tiny dance floor in front of a giant video screen, or have a relatively quiet drink on the outside terrace.

Outside terraces spring up like mushrooms in the summer/autumn months. **La Latina** in the marina and **Varadero**, beside the jetfoil station by the harbour, are where the beautiful people hang out.

If you are looking for something a little more informal in the jeans line, **Toca-**

Toca in the Secretario Artiles is extremely lively at weekends as is its neighbour, **Area**, a disco/bar where they play only Spanish music. The perennially popular **Diseño** in Nicolás Estévanez and **Utopía** in Tomás Miller have maintained their appeal over the years by constantly revising their image. Consider also **Wilson**, Calle Franchy 20, tel: 22 14 10, another lively disco.

If your tastes in music and nightlife are more sedate, adjourn to the piano-bar **La Clave**, in Alfredo Jones, which allows singalongs. And if you want to try your hand

Glitz at Pachá

(and feet) at dancing *sevillanas* and flamenco, try the **Sala Rociero** in the Calle Olof Palme, just round the corner from Plaza de la Victoria. Karaoke clubs/bars have also sprung up around this area.

Pubs with Live Music

Places to check out, in addition to those already mentioned, are: **Bar Polo**, Dr Rafael Gonzalez 2; **Los Lisos**, Paseo de las Canteras and Nicolás Fernández; and **Zorba's**, Luis Morote 51. Most of the bigger hotels have dancing in discos or nightclubs.

Cinemas

The main cinemas are the multiscreen **Royal**, León y Castillo 40, tel: 36 09 54, and **Galaxy**, Mesa y Lopez, tel: 22 44 74

Bar Heineken

– each with six screens – and **Cine Capitol**, Paseo Tomás Morales, tel: 36 61 68.

Other Entertainments

There are occasional shows at **Teatro Pérez Galdós**, Lentini 1, tel: 36 15 09, which hosts big-name international performers as well as the island's symphony and operatic companies. There are lectures, exhibitions and occasionally concerts at the arts centre known as **Centro Insular de Cultura**, Primero de Mayo, tel: 37 21 44.

The South

Down South, where you go depends pretty much on which resort you are staying in, but generally speaking every shopping centre (except Faro 2) has one or two places which are the in-places for the area, where locals come to to sit on the terrace and watch the passing crowds. These change from one year to the next so you must play it by ear – literally.

Recently, the Kasbah's biggest pulls have been **El Garaje** and **Fantasy Island**, whilst in the Plaza shopping centre in Maspalomas it is **Pachá** and **Chic**. People who like to bop until they drop should try **La Roca** (San Agustín), strictly for those with stamina.

Cabaret and Casino

If your taste in nightlife runs to cabaret, try **Voila** at the Meliá Tamarindos Hotel in San Augustín (reservations, tel: 76 68 28), which offers spectacular Las Vegas-style shows.

This hotel also has a **casino** offering roulette, blackjack, chemin du fer, baccarat, and slot machines (men are required to wear a tie and everyone is required to show their passport or identity card to get in).

Casino in Las Palmas

Calendar of Special Events

It is hardly an exaggeration to say that every day is a *fiesta* in Gran Canaria. Celebration of name days, religious feast days, local historical events and ancient traditions are frequent. Rare is the day when fireworks are not going off in one town or another on the island.

Like everything else in Gran Canaria, the local festivities are a peculiar mixture of pagan revelry and Christian solemnity. Celebrations common to the whole of the island may include organised competitions of *lucha canaria* (the traditional Canary wrestling) or displays of local dancing and singing.

If you are lucky enough to attend a fiesta, you'll need plenty of energy. If a celebration begins mid-morning, it is usual to continue partying until the small hours of the next day. The Canary Islanders take their revelry seriously. Carnival, for example, is a sleepless seven-day event that rivals even its equivalent in Río de Janeiro.

January

New Year is a major event all over Spain. In Gran Canaria people celebrate either at home, on the beach with fireworks or in a nightclub or disco where *collones* (special festivities complete with party hats, streamers and silly plastic noses) are organised. However it is celebrated, tradition insists that as the local church bells ring midnight revellers swallow 12 grapes, chime by chime, for good luck over the year ahead, and also consume lots of *cava* (sparkling wine).

On the 5 January islanders buy presents for **Día de Reyes** (the Day of the Three Wise Men) which falls on the 6th. On the evening of the 5th every village and town holds a procession of the Three Wise Men. As the processions are held at different times in different villages, it is possible

Fiesta dress

71

to see up to nine Wise Men on a variety of mounts (camels, donkeys or horses) or even motorised. The 6 January is a national holiday.

February

The main celebration during February is **Carnival**, which usually spans the last week of February and the first week of March, though different parts of the island begin and end at different times (the first celebrations are in Agüimes and the last in Maspalomas).

The period is packed with special events, but in particular look out for the competition of the **Murgas**, bands of strolling singers who specialise in poking fun at local politicians and events; the **Elección de la Reina**, the Carnival Queen contest, usually awash in sequins and feathers; the **Fiesta de la Sábana**, the Sheet Party, when all you need is a sheet plus a little imagination; the different *mogollones*, open-air dances accompanied by *salsa* music; the Carnival Parade and the **Entierro de la Sardina**, the Burial of the Sardine followed by the Widows' Dance, which is possibly the most enjoyable part of the whole Carnival.

March/April

After a month of pagan revelry, 19 March is the Feast of **San José** (St Joseph, and thus Father's Day). Since the Spaniards celebrate their name day, this is one of the most important days on the annual calendar.

Semana Santa, Holy Week leading up to Easter, is an extremely important religious festival in Spain. The most famous celebrations are held in Seville, but the occasion is also taken very seriously in Gran Canaria, with shops and offices closed on Holy Thursday and Good Friday. Processions abound throughout the island.

29 April marks the controversial celebration of the Spanish conquest.

May

1 May is Labour Day (**Día del Trabajo**) with the traditional demonstrations of the trade unions.

The 30 May is the **Día de Canarias**, an official holiday celebrated throughout the Canary Islands to mark the anniversary of the granting of autonomous rule to the archipelago in 1982.

Carnival revellers

June

17 June is the feast day of **Corpus Christi** when streets of various towns and Vegueta in Las Palmas are painstakingly covered with carpets of flowers. The 24th marks the feast of **San Juan**, doubly important since it is also the anniversary of the founding of the city of Las Palmas. A whole week of events is organised, including open-air concerts and folklore. On the night of San Juan, which is the Spaniards' equivalent of Hallowe'en, large bonfires are built, especially on the beaches.

July

The 16th marks the celebrations of the **Fiestas del Carmen**, patron saint of all those who work on the seas who is greatly revered by the Canary islanders. The most moving processions are held in the Puerto de la Luz, La Isleta, Gáldar and Mogán. From the 22–25 July, the most important celebrations for Gáldar and San Bartolomé de Tirajana take place, these being known as the **Fiestas de Santiago el Apóstol**.

August

The other great traditional pagan celebration is held on 4 August: **La Bajada de la Rama** in Agaete. This celebrates one of the rain-making rituals of the *Canarios*.

There is also **La Traida del Agua** in Telde. The 29th is the celebration of the **Virgen de la Cuevita** in Artenara, marked by a torchlit night procession.

September

Possibly the biggest celebration on Gran Canaria is held on 8 September, the **Virgen del Pino** in Teror. Locals make a night-time pilgrimage to Teror, with some of the most devout proceeding on their knees.

The 10 September marks another typical *Canarios'* celebration, the **Fiesta del**

Religious procession

Charco, which takes place in San Nicolás de Tolentino. On this occasion locals try to catch fish with their hands in a specially constructed pool.

October

The **Fiestas de la Naval** are celebrated in La Isleta and the area called La Naval, around 6 October. They celebrate the victory of the Spanish Armada over Sir Francis Drake in 1595. National festivities, consisting mainly of military parades, of the **Día de la Hispanidad** take place on the 12th.

November/December

1 November is **Día de los Difuntos** (All Souls' Day). 6 December is the **Día de la Constitución** (to celebrate the the 1978 Constitution on which democratic Spain is now based). The day is an official holiday, and in Telde, the patron saint, St Gregory, is celebrated with a parade and festival.

The 25th, of course, is **Christmas** when you will come across *belenes* (nativities). In particular, look for the ones in San Gregorio, Telde, in the Museo de Piedras, Ingenio and the 'live' nativity staged in Agaete.

PRACTICAL Information

GETTING THERE

The usual way to reach Gran Canaria is by plane – though you can always opt for the combination of flying to Tenerife, to the Reina Sofía airport and then taking

Inter-island transport

a taxi up to Santa Cruz where you can catch the jetfoil directly to Las Palmas de Gran Canaria. The jetfoil service runs a winter and a summer timetable. To find out when there is a jetfoil available (the travelling time is 1 hour, 20 minutes), phone Trasmediterránea, tel: (928) 454645.

There are lots of charter flights to Gran Canaria. Although it is possible to find flight only deals, it usually works out cheaper to take a package with accommodation included.

The airport at Gandó in Gran Canaria is in the process of being extended to accommodate not only tourists to this island but also those travelling on to Lanzarote or Fuerteventura. If you are travelling under your own steam, you can either take the airport bus to the centre of Las Palmas de Gran Canaria (around 500ptas) or catch a taxi, which will charge a standard price of around 3,500ptas. To travel down south if you are not on a package trip is expensive. Although a regular bus service does exist, it leaves from the far side of the very busy motorway – not the airport itself – and there is no bridge to help you get across. When going out of town by taxi, always get a quote in advance from the driver. The run to Playa del Inglés costs around 7,000ptas.

TRAVEL ESSENTIALS

When to Go

High season (*temporada alta*) begins in October and runs through to April/May. Although it is true to say that Gran Canaria has sun and even temperatures all year round, the best months are September and October, when schools restart in Spain. The south enjoys sunshine all year round, which is why many tour operators have introduced sunshine guarantee clauses in their holiday offers. However, although the weather is beautifully warm in January and February, the water is icy cold.

July and August are months to be avoided if possible since this is when the locals are on holiday themselves and everything is much more crowded. It is also when Las Palmas de Gran Canaria is victim of the *panza de burro* (see *Climate*) which produces intense heat but little real sunshine.

Climate

The average temperature in Gran Canaria is 22°C (72°F) although, as I point out

Year-round sun

throughout this guidebook, the temperature varies according to the altitude. The south in general is rarely overcast, though on the days when there is *viento del sur*, a kind of sirocco, the sky is a dull grey. It is a mistake to think you are quite safe from sunburn on these days, for the ultra-violet rays are trapped between the leaden sky and the beach, producing what the locals call *resol*, 'double sun'.

When the day is windy, the locals avoid the Playa del Inglés and Maspalomas and make for beaches further west, such as Puerto Rico and Taurito, which are more sheltered.

In Las Palmas de Gran Canaria, the *sirocco* brings sand from Morocco, producing a very disagreeable thunderous atmosphere (*polvo en suspensión* – literally 'dust in the air'). People who suffer from allergies should try to head south when this occurs since to stay in the city until the rain rinses away the problem can entail much suffering. When it rains, it rains hard, but only in very short bursts and the temperature remains the same. March and April are the months when the weather is most unsettled, but even then this affects only the higher regions of the island.

Two other phenomena which you should be aware of are the famous *panza de burro* or 'donkey's belly', an enormous grey cloud which settles over the capital of the island in July/August, producing intense heat, and the *mar de nubes* (or 'sea of clouds'). You can climb up above the clouds but any hopes of taking panoramic photographs of the island are ruined. However, neither of these phenomena tend to last more than one day at a time. Rolling mists (and they travel at speed) can also be found on higher ground.

Year-round swimming

Clothing

Coats and jackets are not needed but a light cardigan or pullover is necessary if you are intending to travel up to higher regions. Sunglasses are a must and a pair of plastic sandals for use on some of the beaches is a good idea since there may be rocks underfoot.

Sensible footwear is necessary if you are thinking of walking around to any great extent and some kind of head protection is also important. Men should take a tie if they intend visiting the casino. Umbrellas are not worth packing; in the rare case of needing one, you will find they are sold dirt cheap in the Corte Inglés in Las Palmas.

Documents

You need a valid passport and an international driving licence if you plan on hiring a car. You should also take out some kind of travel insurance to safeguard against accidents and pick up the E111 form from your local post office before leaving home; this entitles EU citizens to free medical treatment.

Electricity

The electricity supply is 220 volts, and the Spaniards use round two-pin sockets, so UK visitors will need an adaptor for any electrical appliances. Four-star and five-star hotels provide hairdriers. Laundry services are cheap and often preferable to the results of a travel iron.

Time Differences

There is an hour's difference between mainland Spain and the Canary Islands. Gran Canaria is one hour ahead of GMT, but when the clocks change they may be two hours ahead for a week or so.

with the rest of Spain. With full integration of Spain and the Canary Islands in the EU, locals believe that their cost of living will suffer.

Parties of a nationalist nature have sprung up over the last few years. One of these in particular, ATI, has had so much success that it holds the balance of power in a regional coalition government with the Socialist party, PSOE.

Population and Religion

There is a great ethnic mix in Gran Canaria. People from all parts of the world have come here for business or pleasure and stayed to become fully integrated in society. Thus all religions have been represented here for some time. The Templo Ecuménico in the south holds multilingual religious ceremonies. There is also a mosque in the Yumbo shopping centre in the south and various churches of the Latter-Day Saints scattered over the island.

GETTING ACQUAINTED

Geography

The Canary archipelago is on latitude 28° and comprises seven inhabited islands, an eighth which is partially inhabited (La Graciosa), four or five uninhabited islands (Lobos, Montaña Clara, Alegranza, Roque del Este, Roque del Oeste) and another mythical island, San Borondón (St Brendan's), which appears and disappears at will.

The seven islands are divided between two provinces: Las Palmas which includes Gran Canaria, Fuerteventura, Lanzarote, La Graciosa (and the uninhabited islands) and Tenerife which takes in Tenerife, La Palma, El Hierro and La Gomera.

People in Gran Canaria are very touchy about visitors confusing them with the Balearic Islands or with Tenerife.

Government and Economy

The Canary Islands have an autonomous regional government with fully devolved powers in very limited fields. The economy, which was formerly dependent upon agriculture, began to rely heavily on tourism in the 1960s. This industry now represents almost 80 percent of the archipelago's total income.

At times, the Canary islanders have protested that the central government in Spain is insensitive to their situation as isolated islands. Since most products are imported, the cost of living is high compared

MONEY MATTERS

It is best to come with peseta traveller's cheques and local currency. Money changers are many and their rates differ widely. Avoid *bureaux de change* in hotels if possible, for they tend to offer poor rates. Always try to change money in banks (open from 9am–2pm, closed Saturday).

Some banks have currency exchange points (eg Caja de Madrid in Calle Albareda) similar to cash machines outside their premises. These are not recommended except when all other options are closed.

Credit cards are widely accepted, above all American Express and Visa. Cash points in the area of El Puerto are usually housed inside booths, for obvious reasons, and allow you to carry out your transactions in the language of your choice.

Remember the harbour area suffers from all the typical problems of such a district, so do not display money or valuables and don't carry wallets in back pockets. A money belt or pouch is a wise investment.

Tipping

Perhaps expected in restaurants and hairdressers but not elsewhere. Ten percent is the norm.

GETTING AROUND

Las Palmas de Gran Canaria with over 400,000 inhabitants is almost worse to drive in than London. People use their cars for absolutely everything and want to park right next to their destination. Since the city was originally planned for a small number of vehicles and it is esti-

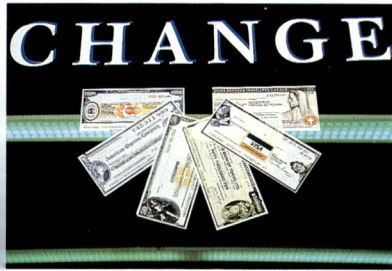

mated that there is an average of at least two cars per person of driving age in the capital, the effect is bedlam. For inner-city travel I suggest you use the *guaguas* (buses), which are cheap (125ptas) and cheerful. A *bono guagua* (pronounced bo-neoh wawa) which can be used for 10 journeys costs 750ptas and can be bought in any bank.

Taxis are good value with the longest run in the city costing only around 500ptas. Walking is only pleasant in Las Palmas in pedestrian areas such as Vegueta, the Avenida Marítima or around Las Canteras.

To travel around the island you can use the green buses, the SALCAI (tel: 38 11 10 for information), which run a particularly fast line down to the south, or the UTINSA (tel: 36 83 35) which tend to be slower and serve rural areas. Both services leave from the Estacion de Guaguas, Avenida Rafael Cabrera, tel: 36 10 79 (across from the Parque San Telmo), as do all bus services including local buses.

However, the easiest way to travel round the island is by car, especially since the introduction of colourful new signposting. You can hire anything from a Seat Panda to a Mitsubishi mini-van seating nine. Rates range upwards from about 2,500ptas per day and are much the same at all companies, but have a more reliable service than others (Avis is a good

Winding roads

bet). There is a larger variety of vehicles to choose from outside the airport. Be careful not to park in prohibited zones – tow trucks operate constantly.

For organised excursions, Tamaragua (tel: 27 20 00) in Nicolás Estévanez and in the south, or any of the branches of Ultramar Express (tel: 27 30 22) offer you everything from shark-fishing to belly-dancing at competitive prices.

Various ferries (information, tel: 22 70 75) run between the islands from the port of Las Palmas. Trasmediterránea (tel: 26 00 70) operates jetfoils to Tenerife, a trip that takes 80 minutes. The same company also runs ferries to Fuerteventura and Lanzarote. The Fred Olsen Shipping Line (tel: 46 48 00) has daily departures from Puerto de las Nieves (near Agaete) to Tenerife. Ferries which take cars serve all the islands. There is also an excellent inter-island flight service (tel: 57 42 20/25 41 40) for information), but remember that flights are heavily booked at Christmas, Easter and in July/August. Book in any travel agency. Naysa S.A. (Avenida Ramirez Bethencourt 10, tel: 36 10 44) operates an aero-taxi.

Car and Bike Rentals

Autos Beltran: Apts Solymar near foot of Avenida Tirajana, Playa del Inglés, tel: 76 42 66, fax: 77 29 90. Cars from 2,000ptas per day.
Autos Nanicar: Avenida Tirajana 14 (next

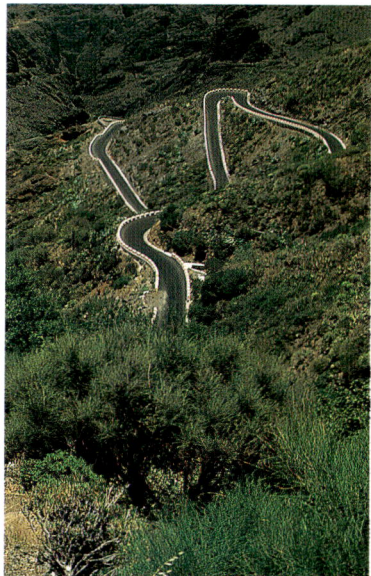

to Hotel Rey Carlos), Playa del Inglés, tel: 76 11 30, fax: 77 16 44. Cars from 2,500ptas per day.

Autos Perez: Sol Bardinos Hotel, Las Palmas, tel: 26 11 36, fax: 26 55 32; Avenida Tenerife 8, Playa del Inglés, tel: 76 36 16. From 3,000ptas per day.

Caribe Cars: Avenida Tirajana 9, Playa del Inglés, tel: 76 60 61. Cars from 2,300ptas per day.

Europcar: Tomás Miller 63, Las Palmas, tel: 26 36 97, fax: 22 85 06; Edificio Bayuca, Playa del Inglés, tel: 76 55 00. From 5,000ptas per day.

Moto & Bike: Gran Chaparral, Playa del Inglés, tel: 77 33 31. Bicycles from 900ptas per day, also scooters and motorbikes.

Orlando: at airport, tel: 78 32 22; Calle Viriato and Guanartema, Las Palmas, tel: 26-73-76; Playa del Inglés, Avenida Tirajana 23, tel: 76 55 08. From 2,500ptas per day, 7,000ptas per week

Rent a Trike: Edificio Tanife, Playa del Inglés, tel: 970 840 233. Three-wheeled monsters.

Sunfun Motorbike Rental: Gran Chaparral, Avenida Gran Canaria, Playa del Inglés, tel: /fax: 76 38 29. From 2,000ptas per day.

Avis (tel: 57 43 04) and **Hertz** (tel: 57 45 54) both have airport counters as well as rental offices in Las Palmas centre.

Tours

In Playa del Inglés, many travel/tour agencies are located at the top end of Avenda Tirajana. These include: **Montana**, tel: 76 00 12); **Canary Travel**; tel: 77 47 12; **Suntourist S.L.**, tel: 76 64 89; **Calipso Tourist**, tel: 76 15 52; and **Miguel's Jeep Safari** at the Eurocentre: tel: 76 48 96 . There are a number of timeshare companies operating which offer free trips in return for inspecting their properties. These are legal but should be regarded with caution.

HOURS & HOLIDAYS

The people in the Canary Islands work according to two timetables: one for the so-called summer and the other for the rest of the year. Most of the time, life is geared to schedules on mainland Spain.

Schools start at 8–8.30am (take note if your hotel/apartment is near a school), but there are so many children of school age (although the birthrate in the Canary Islands has fallen) that high school students are taught in shifts and may still be at their desks at 8pm.

Offices are supposed to open at about 9am but few make it before 9.30, apart from the banks, some of which begin at 8.30am. Shops open around 10am, which is the time El Corte Inglés opens, although food shops are open earlier. They close again at 2pm and reopen around 4pm. Everything closes around 8pm though you will find places in Las Canteras which stay open later.

The summer timetable is applied by offices such as the Tourist Information Office, in the months of July and August, due to lack of staff. In those months offices open from 9am–2pm and do not reopen in the afternoon.

The people of Gran Canaria do not take a *siesta*. In fact, they do not appear to sleep very much at all, which possibly explains the slow rhythm all through the day. Nightlife rarely begins until around midnight and continues well into the morning.

Taxis are available 24 hours a day and the airport is also open all night.

Remember that public holidays (see *Calendar of Special Events*) are kept religiously – only restaurants and some bars do not close. If the holiday falls on a Thursday, Friday is also taken as a holiday. People all over Spain are experts at inventing *puentes*, ie long weekends.

ACCOMMODATION

Generally speaking, the accommodation in the south of the island is of excellent standard and offers possibilities for all pockets. Las Palmas de Gran Canaria tends to cater more for business people than for tourists *per se* and accommodation divides between the very good and the very bad with little in between. Since people no longer tend to stay the whole time in Las Palmas but go south for the sunshine, lots of the hotels have become rather rundown.

In the capital, the best hotels cost around 20,000ptas per night whilst more modest, yet decent accommodation costs 5,000 and 10,000ptas per night. In the following recommendations $ indicates accommodation under 5,000 ptas, $$ is under 20,000ptas, and $$$ over 20,000ptas. All price guides are for a double room.

Las Palmas

Hotel Santa Catalina (tel: 243040, $$$) is possibly the most expensive of the hotels in Las Palmas, clocking in at a minimum of 40,000ptas per night, but worth it. On **Las Canteras** itself, however, there is a wide choice to suit all tastes. **Hotel Imperial Playa** (tel: 4464854, $$) which belongs to the NH chain is, like most, a refurbished old hotel with wonderful views and magnificent rooms. **Hotel Meliá** (tel: 267600, $$), **Reina Isabel** (tel: 260100,

$$) and the **Hotel Sansofé** (tel: 224062, $$) are also on the beachfront.

Within a block or two of Playa Las Canteras are many more places to stay. In ascending order of price, they include: **Pensione Princessa**, Princessa Guayarmina 2 (tel: 467704, $); **Residence Alva**, Alfredo Jones 29, opposite the Reina Isabel (tel: 264232, $), which is suitable for week-long stays or more; **Hotel El Cisne**, Ferreras 19, one block from the beach, opposite Hyper Dino supermarket (tel: 468820, $); **Hotel Concorde**, Tomás Miller 85, near the Reina Isabel (tel: 262730, fax: 265774, $$); **Hotel Cantur**, Sagasta 28 (tel: 273000, fax: 272373, $$); **Hotel Atlanta**, Alfredo Jones 37, also near the Reina Isabel (tel: 255062, fax: 273485, $$); **Astoria Hotel**, Fernando Guanarteme (tel: 54225750, fax: 272499, $$); and **Hotel Tennesoya**, Sagasta 98, (tel: 469608, fax: 460279, $$).

Further towards the centre are **Sol Inn Bardinos**, Eduardo Benot 3 (tel: 266100, fax: 229139, $$$), incorporating a circular tower with 26th floor swimming pool, and the **Hotel Parque**, Parque San Telmo (tel: 368000, $$).

Possibly the best bet if you want to do your own thing, are the apartments **Colón Playa** (tel: 265954, $) on the beachfront at the end of Alfredo Jones, which offer seaviews and a central position.

The South

Down south, you can choose between a number of resorts with different characters and different types of accommodation.

In Playa del Inglés, your options include **BarbaCan**, Avenida Tirajana 27 (tel: 772030, fax: 761852), a complex of apartments and bungalows around a gigantic pool, with restaurant and bar. Decent hotels in Playa del Inglés are: **Hotel Rey Carlos**, Avenida Tirajana 14, (tel: 760106, fax: 762945), with a lush, tropical atmosphere, good food and a pool (see *Itinerary 8*), and **Palm Beach Hotel**, Avenida Menceyes (tel: 772726, fax: 767252, $$–$$$). **Hotel Beverly Park**, on the seafront (tel: 774042), with three pools, restaurants and bars, costs just £350 per week in April (£700 or more in December) for half board. Also good value is **Hotel Par-**

que **Tropical** (tel: 760712, *$$*), which is beautifully designed and central.

The best hotel if you are staying in Maspalomas is the **Oasis**, with double rooms either looking onto the Oasis or onto the sea. Either way, the view is beautiful. Rooms here costs around 40,000ptas for a double. There's also the **Palm Beach Hotel** (cousin of the one in Playa del Inglés) on Avenida del Oasis (tel: 721032, fax: 141808, *$$$*).

As big and well accoutred as the others listed, but in quieter San Augustín, is **Hotel Gloria Palace**, Las Margaritas (tel:768304, fax 767929), costing 13,000ptas in April–June, 17,000ptas most of the rest of year.

Patalavaca, just round the corner from Arguineguín, offers the **Steigenberg Canaria** (tel: 150400, *$$*) with incredible sunset vistas. In Mogán, the beautiful **Club de Mar** complex (little Venice) costs a very decent 10,000ptas (tel: 740100, *$$*).

Budget and Rural Accommodation

You can find apartments and bungalows to suit all pockets. Consult the travel agencies mentioned in *Getting Around* or in El Corte Inglés, Las Palmas. Camping is another option, but sites tend to be noisy (ev-

Typical tiling

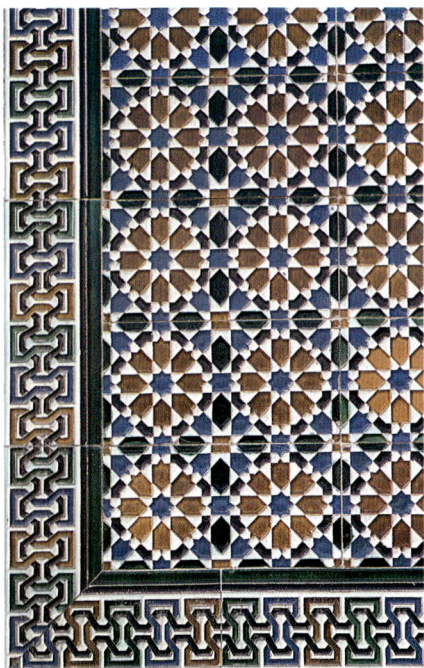

erybody takes their TV), crowded and with few facilities. They are good for meeting people, however, and for travellers on shoestring budgets. (Information from the campsites at Pasito Blanco and Taurito.)

Gran Canaria has been developing what it likes to call 'rural tourism', whose genesis was the mdernisation of a network of old tracks or pathways which were once the only means of reaching some of the remoter villages. Now that almost all are connected with an efficient system of highways, old homesteads and farms have been developed into hostels or *pensiones* which offer an attractive alternative to big hotels in busy resorts.

In the region of Vega de San Mateo, near Cruz de Tejeda at the highest point of the island, for example, are several properties owned by the Rural Tourism Association including an aboriginal cave dwelling carved out of the mountainside, a two-storey country house and El Vinco, a renovated 300-year-old home with period furniture. Inquiries about these can be made direct to RETUER, Lourdes 2, Vega de San Mateo, 35320 Gran Canaria, tel: 661668, fax: 661560.

There are many similar dwellings in various parts of the island. A fully illustrated booklet listing all such places is available from the Patronato de Turismo, Gran Canaria (fax: 929-362822).

HEALTH & EMERGENCIES

Should you need attention for anything more serious than insect bites, sunburn or a gippy stomach, you should make for the emergency services (*Urgencias*) in any of the following hospitals: Clínica del Pino in the Calle Tomás Morales (tel: 23 11 99), the Materno-Infantil (principally maternity and children's hospital but attends all kinds of cases and ages), Avenida Marítima del Sur (tel: 32 03 33) or the Hospital Insular, also in the Avenida Marítima (tel: 31 30 33), in Las Palmas de Gran Canaria. These are the hospitals which look after the general population. There are usually English-speaking doctors and nurses around, but if you need to explain your problem without misunderstanding of any kind, then your best bet is to make for the Hospital Inglés, Paseo de la Cornisa, 1 (tel: 25 42 43) which, as its name indicates, has English-speaking staff. Also worth knowing about is Inter Clinic, Calle Sagasta 62 (tel: 278 826), where there is 24-hour access to doctors, dentists and X-rays and they specialise in treating foreign (European) nationals with medical travel insurance.

In Maspalomas, EC citizens can use free of charge the medical services of Cruce del Tablero (tel: 14 20 78) after filling the form E111. Clinics in Playa del Inglés include the Suomi British Clinic, Edificio Buenos Aires (tel: 76 27 42) and Health Centre Canarias, Avenida Tirajana (tel: 76 17 96). Dentists are Dr Luis Pereda Otero, Sargentos Provisionales 14, Playa del Inglés (tel: 76 70 37) and Dr Maya Caceres, Lanzarote 23, San Ferando, (tel: 76 75 73).

Do not drink the water from the tap under any circumstances. Try to avoid it even for brushing your teeth and eschew ice in your drinks. Bottled water comes in two types, *con* (with) or *sin* (without) *gas*. Buy this in supermarkets as bars inflate prices. Should you be caught by a dose of diarrhoea, ask for Fortasec in the chemist's and avoid drinking alcohol for at least six hours. One tablet does the trick.

Try to avoid over-exposure to the sun. Keep out of direct sunlight from 1–4pm and watch out for children catching double dosage in the water. Acute sunburn or sunstroke should be treated in hospital.

Crime

The people of Gran Canaria are generally peaceful and law-abiding but, as happens in any big city with a busy harbour area, there are incidents of bag-snatching and theft. Do not court trouble and only carry your passport and other papers around when absolutely necessary, ie when changing money. In Las Palmas, the area beyond and behind the Sansofé hotel is not particularly safe at night and is perfectly easy to avoid. The same can be said of Ripoche.

The south is not free from these problems either, especially its bungalows, which are less well protected than other types of accommodation. Should you have problems contact the nearest *comisaría* (police station). Sometimes, you may need to ask your consulate for help, as not all police stations have interpreting services. For emergencies of any kind, dial 091. The national police number is 76 40 00.

CULTURAL EVENTS

The Canary islanders have always felt culturally disadvantaged compared with their fellow countrymen, though unnecessarily so. Consequently a great deal of effort is made to compensate, with many cultural events.

An esteemed International Festival of Classical Music is held every February (tickets and programmes from SOCAEM well in advance to avoid disappointment; tel: 291944/292588). The annual Opera Festival is held in March/April and two music festivals, Atlantida and Womad, entice audiences in January and November respectively.

Travelling theatre groups regularly appear at the Teatro Pérez Galdós. The University of Las Palmas de Gran Canaria organises various courses throughout the year (see newspapers for details) and a summer school every August, with speakers from all parts of the world. The CAAM also organises excellent seminars to coincide with their exhibitions.

Sunset over Roque Nublo, with Tenerife's Mt Teide in the distance

MUSEUMS

The following museums are all in Las Palmas and form the basis of *Itinerary 6*:

CASA DE COLON
Colon 1
Tel: 31 23 73
Weekdays 9am–6pm, weekends 9am–3pm. Beautiful, 12-room house set around twin courtyards with models of Las Palmas in different eras, nautical maps, navigational instruments and charts of Columbus's journeys, paintings on loan from Madrid's Prado museum, and two noisy parrots guarding an ancient well.

CASA MUSEO PEREZ GALDOS
Cano 6
Tel: 36 69 76
Weekdays 9am–1pm and 4–8pm. Among the rooms is a reproduction of Galdós's Santander study with furniture designed by the author and playwright, and hundreds of books, his own and those of Goethe, Dickens, Balzac, Tolstoy and Zola, many autographed by their authors.

MUSEUM OF RELIGIOUS ART
Espíritu Santo
Tel: 20, 31 49 89
Weekdays 9am–1.30pm, and 4–6.30pm, Saturday 9am–2pm. Half a dozen rooms containing portraits and religious artifacts, the foremost of which, the pinewood and volcanic rock treasure room, stores silk and damask vestments and 16th-century wooden sculptures.

CENTRO ATLANTICO DE ARTE MODERNO
Calle de Los Balcones 9
Tel: 31 18 24
Tuesday to Saturday 10am–9pm, Sunday 10am–2pm. Concentrates on the work of young Canarian artists.

MUSEO CANARIO
Calle Dr. Chil 25
Tel: 31 56 00
Weekdays 10am–8pm, weekends 10am–2pm. The famous Guanche mummies, not too well preserved, are on display in glass cases upstairs along with row after row of unadorned Cro Magnon skulls.

MUSEO NESTOR
Parque Doramas
Tel: 24 51 35
Tuesday–Friday 10am–1pm and 4–8pm, Sunday 11am–2pm. Well-lit, two-storey space with antique bookcases; a dress from a 1934 production of *Cavalleria Rusticana*, for which Néstor did the sets; his sketches for the Pérez Galdós theatre; and numerous paintings and posters from his relatively short life.

CHILDREN'S ATTRACTIONS

PALMITOS PARK
Tel: 14 02 76
Tropical garden with birds and butterflies. Open daily 9.30am–6pm. Bus 45 from Playa del Inglés

SIOUX CITY
Tel: 76 25 73
Western frontier town theme park. From 9am daily except Monday. Show and barbecue 6pm Friday. Bus 29 from Playa del Inglés.

RANCHO PARK
Playa del Inglés
Tel: 14 20 10
Horses for hire, riding lessons. Daily 10am–midnight.

AQUA SUR
On Palmitos Park road
Tel: 14 05 25
Water park open daily from 10am.

OCEAN PARK
Campo Internacional de Maspalomas
Tel: 76 43 61
Water park open daily 10am–5pm.

MUNDO ABORIGEN,
On Fataga road
Tel: 77 30 80
Depicts the island's aborigines. .Bus 18 from Playa del Inglés.

SUBMARINE ADVENTURE
Puerto de Mogán
Tel: 56 51 08
Underwater excursions. Bus 32 from Playa del Inglés.

GRAN KARTING CLUB
On the road to Las Palmas from Playa del Inglés
Tel: 76 00 90

REPTILANDIA PARK
On the Gáldar–Agaete highway
Tel: 55 12 69
Daily 11am– 5.30pm. Bus 103 from Las Palmas.

COCODRILOS PARK
Los Corralillos, Villa de Agüimes
Tel: 78 47 25
Hundreds of wild animals. Daily 10am–6pm. Bus 21 from Las Palmas.

SPORT

The south of the island is the place for water sports, with lessons in water-skiing, diving, underwater fishing, windsurfing (generally regarded as the best in the world) and sailing all on offer. The best place for these, and for shark fishing, is Puerto Rico.

If you want to go your own way and don't need tuition then Pozo Izquierdo is the best place for windsurfing (signposted on the road down to the south, around Arinaga). The world championship heats were held here only recently. Playa del Aguila, just before San Agustín and Bahía Feliz are also good for windsurfing. For ordinary surfers, the area around Bañaderos and the end of the Canteras beach, beside the road out to the north, are the best places.

Vela latina (a highly skilful type of sailing) is not easy to understand but very popular with the natives (the sport generates a lot of betting). *Lucha canaria* (Canary wrestling) may be programmed to celebrate special events and is very exciting to watch – as are the *lucha del garrote or juego del garrote* ('crook' fighting) competitions.

The football season begins in September – but visiting spectators should avoid matches between U D Las Palmas and Tenerife, which are well known for their violence. The international car racing championship rally is held in the Jinámar Valley near Telde every year.

Golf: Bandama Golf Club, Santa Brigída, tel: 35 10 50, with restaurant (see *Itinerary 3*); Maspalomas Golf Club, Avenida de Africa, behind Maspalomas Dunes, tel: 76 25 81, near hotels and restaurants (see *Itinerary 8*).

Marinas: Las Palmas Yachting Harbour, tel: 24 41 01 – moorings for hire; Pasito Blanco Marina, Maspalomas, tel: 14 21 94 – moorings, watersports, deep-sea fishing, skin diving; Puerto Rico Yachting Harbour, tel: 56 11 41 – moorings, watersports, deep-sea fishing; Mogán Yachting Harbour, Puerto de Mogán, tel: 56 56 68 – moorings, deep-sea fishing.

Sailing: Provincial Sailing Federation, León y Castillo 244, Las Palmas, tel: 29 15 67; Anfi del Mar-Molina Sport, Mogán, tel: 15 07 98.

Surfing/Windsurfing: Puerto Rico Sailing School, tel: 56 07 72; Club Mistral Bahía Feliz, Tarajillo Beach, tel: 77 40 25.

Horseback Riding: Bandama Golf Club Riding School, Santa Brigída, tel: 35 12 90.

Flying/Parachuting: Gran Canaria Aeroclub, highway to the south 46km, tel: 76 24 47; Paraclub of Gran Canaria, León y Castillo 244, Las Palmas, tel: 24 73 93.

Tennis/Squash: Most big hotels have courts with night play facilities.

MAPS

In addition to the pull-out map that accompanies this guide, pick up the excellent free maps available in El Corte Inglés in Las Palmas. The Tourist Information office (Parque Santa Catalina) can also provide you with detailed maps.

TOILETS

Unlike on mainland Spain, toilets in bars and restaurants are generally well-tended. Don't use the toilets in the Parque Santa Catalina, however, or any other public toilet.

Lack of toilets is one of the handicaps of Carnival merrymaking. The portable loos provided are grossly insufficient. Your best option is to pop into a bar – nobody will object.

COMMUNICATIONS & NEWS
Telephone

For long-distance phone calls try to use telephone booths or exchanges. If you can possibly avoid it, try not to phone from hotels, since their charges are considerably more. The prefix for Tenerife and province is 922. The prefix for Gran Canaria is 928.

To dial other countries (Canada follows the US system) first dial the international access code 00, then the country code: Australia (61); France (33); Germany (49); Italy (39); Japan (81); Netherlands (31); UK (44); US (1).

If using a US credit phone card, dial the company's access number: Sprint, tel: 900 99 0013; AT&T, tel: 900 99 00 11; MCI, tel: 900 99 0014.

Newspapers

Gran Canaria has three newspapers – *Canarias 7*, *La Provincia* and *Diario de Las Palmas*. All major European daily newspapers are on the news stands the day following publication.

USEFUL ADDRESSES
Tourist Information

SPANISH NATIONAL TOURIST OFFICE
22–23 Manchester Square,
London W1M
Tel: (0171) 486 8077

OFICINA DE TURISMO
Parque Santa Catalina, Las Palmas
Tel: 26 46 23
Fax: 22 98 20

There are additional tourist offices at Gando airport (tel: 57 40 58); in Playa del Inglés, in the Yumbo shopping centre (tel: 77 15 50); and in Puerto Rico (tel: 56 00 29).

Consulates

All foreign consulates are in Las Palmas:

FRANCE
Calle Néstor de la Torre, 12
Tel: 29 23 71

GERMANY
Franchy Roca 5
Tel: 27 57 00

HOLLAND
León y Castillo 244
Tel: 24 23 82

ITALY
León y Castillo 281
Tel: 24 19 11

JAPAN
S. Rusenor 12
Tel: 32 23 48

PORTUGAL
Franchy Roca 9
Tel: 27 86 12

SWITZERLAND
Dr. Rivero 2
Tel: 27 45 44.

UNITED KINGDOM
Luis Morote 6
Tel: 26 26 58

UNITED STATES
Franchy Roca 5
Tel: 27 12 59

FURTHER READING

Insight Guide: Gran Canaria, Lanzarote and Fuerteventura (revised 1999), provides excellent background reading as well as information on all the sights and a comprehensive travel tips section.

If you are interested in exploring the island by foot, the Sunflower Countryside Guide, *Landscapes of Gran Canaria* by Noel Rochford, provides a sensible and comprehensive selection of walking tours, some of which form part of the Tourist Board's new project to restore the *caminos reales* (royal routes) which linked towns before the island's roads were developed. You can find these guides in most bookshops. For culture vultures, the CAAM (El Centro Atlantico de Arte Moderno) publishes all its catalogues in bilingual (English/Spanish) editions.

Index

THE HOME
MAINTENANCE
MANUAL
SIMON JAMES

SPHERE

SPHERE BOOKS LIMITED
30/32 Gray's Inn Road, London WC1X 8JL

Art & Photo Credits

Photography	**Paul Young** *and*
Pages 10, 11, 12, 13, 14T, 34T, 47T, 74	**Andrew Eames**
5B, 26, 33, 80	**Wolfgang Fritz**
25, 66T, 72	**Tulio Gatti**
35, 53T, 64, 67B, 68, 75B, 76, 77B, 78	**Roger Hilton**
66	**Sergio Rodriguez Matos**
27, 32B, 38, 43B, 52B, 54, 56B, 61, 70	**Gary John Norman**
59T, 63B, 65, 79	**Nigel Tisdall**
71	**Bill Wassman**
Handwriting	**V. Barl**
Production Editor	**Erich Meyer**
Cover Design	**Klaus Geisler**
Cartography	**Berndtson & Berndtson**